be nice

and get what you really want

Best wishes —

By

Lauren Archibeque

Lauren Archibeque

Written by: Lauren Archibeque
Printed in the United States of America
First Printing: June 2018

Published by Sojourn Publishing LLC
In
The United States of America

ISBN: 978-1-62747-124-4 Paperback
ISBN: 978-1-62747-126-8 E-Book

Cover photography by Christine Lowell Photography

Dedication

This is dedicated to Mom …
I will remember everyday …
"This is not a crisis, it's an adventure!"
Your lessons live on.

Table of Contents

Introduction

This book has been years in the making. The writing and editing portion was actually the quick part. The lessons took a lifetime of learning and striving to move out of my own way.

I was not always nice. I had a very angry stage where I actually learned a lot about why not nice doesn't actually work out very well. I went through a stage where I was more manipulative than I like to admit. Using flattery and insincerity as a tool to get what I wanted in the moment. I quickly found that to be not only unsustainable, but detrimental to my own well-being.

I have spent literally decades fine tuning myself and constantly learning. I am a self-development junkie. There is so much information out there to explore! There is always more progress to be made. I am still peeling the onion as they say. Always striving to be more of what I already am - which is a perfectly imperfect human being.

I am not broken and neither are you. We are here to learn and here to grow. And that is what you are doing as you start this next chapter in your life.

My hope is that this book helps you move a little further up your path with ease.

Chapter 1
Why be nice?

Nice has its own gravitational pull. People will want to be in your space and they will want to help you achieve your goals. It's like your own personal version of a spell. There is a reason we say that a woman is bewitching or that a speaker is spell-binding. They have that magic ingredient and they radiate it. In a word, they are nice! Nice to be around, nice to listen to and nice to interact with. You feel safe in their space.

Being nice makes the game of life easier. It reduces stress by convincing others to rally with you. You travel through life with more grace. I love the definition in *Gift from the Sea* by Anne Morrow Lindbergh. I am paraphrasing a little here: "By grace I mean an inner harmony, which can be translated into outward harmony. I am seeking perhaps what Socrates asked for in a prayer when he said, 'May the outward and inward man be at one.'"

Calm, cool and collected are words that fit when we operate from a space of grace. It is as if all things are balanced and smooth. All of the moving parts in life ebb and flow with ease when we are in a state of grace, whereas when we drop out of that state, things that usually are second nature seem challenging.

Stress reduction is an automatic result of being nice. When you are supported by other people who truly want you to succeed, you will find there are infinite ways to create the life you dream about.

Pastor Chon Pugh from Bethlehem Lutheran Church in Mesa, Arizona, created the term God's Math to describe what I am talking about. Chon is a minister and a spirit-led life coach. She pictures that God or the Universe has its own math system in play for us. If it is of God, it multiplies. Positive things automatically multiply using God's Math … things like love, faith, charity, kindness, generosity, gratitude, and basic human niceness are amplified, magnified and multiplied. If it is not of God, it divides. Things like anger, hate, intolerance, impatience, and fear are divisive. I think that is a brilliant way of thinking about how we show up and how Universal Laws show up as well.

When you are pleasant, it pulls other nice people into your life. The Universe provides a padding of soft places to fall when you are in alignment with your purpose and are playing nice with others.

How many times have you read stories where one small nicety completely changed a person's life? People have embellished one version of a story entitled "A Simple

Gesture," told by John W. Schlatter and published in the 1993 bestseller *Chicken Soup for the Soul*. It is the story of how one nice gesture of one teenager helping another pick up some dropped books saved a nerdy boy from carrying out his plan to take his own life. The story has been embellished and re-circulated, but the message is the same. You may never know the end result of being nice in the small moments of each day.

Being pleasant is actually very profitable. Not that you are nice to manipulate people into giving you stuff, but somehow when you are in a place of kindness and acceptance of what is going on, people just naturally want to help you. You get the room upgrade or the discount that you didn't even know about, or you make contact with the exact right person that has the skill set you are looking for, or someone gives you a book that is perfect for where you are in your journey.

Recently, I read a little news article referencing a passenger on American Airlines who had purchased tickets to fly on non-refundable tickets. Unfortunately, he became sick before his scheduled departure date and was advised by his doctor to skip the trip until he was well. Instead of griping and complaining and demanding compensation of some kind, he penned a very humorous letter beginning with "Dear most kind and benevolent American Airlines

Customer Service Staff member," and asking for mercy and sympathy regarding the customary $200 change fee the airline charges to change flights. The airline accommodated his request and sent a very pleasant reply.

In a word, he was nice. He was lighthearted and funny. You can picture that whoever read the letter would have had a smile on their face taking in his very obvious attempt to persuade them to cut him some slack. And in return American Airlines was nice. They waived the fee, giving him a great experience.

My definition of nice is that nice moves you forward and supports others to move forward as well. It pulls the energy up. It brings a spirit of cooperation and comradery to any situation, large or small.

There are a multitude of ways to practice nice in your daily experience: Smiling at a complete stranger, listening with full attention when your child wants to talk about their day, genuinely engaging that cashier in the supermarket, displaying patience when the bank teller can't quite get that computer to cooperate, keeping your composure when your spouse forgets to make the mortgage payment, saying thank you for small things throughout the day. These are all simple acts and can literally change lives. These help move people forward, including you. The energy always shifts when you practice nice.

Nice makes life so much easier and much more fun and fulfilling. Nice is a way to stay true to yourself as you pursue your purpose while living on this planet with all these other humans doing the same thing. Some are more conscious than others. Some of those operating in the highest vibrations are those in hot pursuit of their true life purpose and they incorporate niceness not only as a way of being but also as a way of staying in forward movement. Nice helps other humans interact in ways that will keep progress moving at a great clip.

If we are nice with each other as we go, life is a lot more pleasant and we can all ascend to the heights we dream of attaining. Nice plays! That kind of has a ring to it doesn't it? Win-win comes to mind and win-win is great! It's being nice!

Chapter 2

What is nice?

N ice! What does that even mean?

So much meaning wrapped up in one little word: Pleasant, kind, respectable, good-looking, accomplished, subtle … and the list goes on when you look at a dictionary definition. In our minds, we each conjure up our own picture. How many different ways can the word be used and defined in the world outside of Webster's?

"That's nice, dear." The universal spousal reply when you are not really listening and just want to go back to your relaxing paper or in this day and age, scanning Facebook or watching YouTube videos of funny puppies.

If you talk to my teenagers for more than a few minutes you will most likely hear it used as a verb. "Alex, dinner will be ready in ten minutes." His response? "Nice!" Or is that being used as an adjective? Is "nice" describing dinner or is it responding to the idea that it will be ready shortly? I confuse myself easily.

"Nice throw!" may be heard at a baseball game. It could be sincere or possibly sarcastic, depending on the tone.

"Be nice ..." could be a parental admonition or a general suggestion. "Be nice! His nose isn't that big!" or "Be nice to your sister. She's having a hard day."

Nice is a four-letter word to some people. I have heard a nasty rumor that nice is just another word for doormat. Kind may better describe the type of effect I am talking about and yet somehow I cannot get my mind around the word kind. It sounds old-fashioned to me and brings to mind ladies in long dresses with bonnets carrying parasols. Not that that's a bad thing, it just feels outdated. In some dictionaries "kind" is part of the definition for nice and "nice" is part of the definition of kind.

If you hear the word nice as a negative, I respectfully ask that you either quietly and gently replace the word nice throughout the book with the word kind ... or quit reading right now. So make up your mind pronto because if you continue to read and gripe internally every time you see the word nice ... well ... that's not nice! Not nice for you and not nice for me. Not to mention that all that negative energy just runs amok, which is not beneficial for the world at large. Are we good? Okay ... let's continue.

You may have heard it said that nice guys finish last. Not true! The quote is a farce. As one of my editors kindly noted, going back to its origins, it is based on a punctuation error! (As you can imagine, editors love to share these facts and personally I am grateful).

People have been saying "nice guys finish last" for decades as if it were a real quote from some incredible guru dated to the beginning of time. It is not true.

In his autobiography, *Nice Guys Finish Last* (1975), baseball manager Leo Durocher recounts where the saying originated and how it got twisted by reporters who quoted him.

"The Giants, led by Mel Ott, began to come out of their dugout to take their warm-up. Without missing a beat, I said, "Take a look at that Number Four there. A nicer guy never drew breath than that man there." I called off his players' names as they came marching up the steps behind him, "Walker Cooper, Mize, Marshall, Kerr, Gordon, Thomson. Take a look at them. All nice guys. They'll finish last. Nice guys. Finish last." I said, "They lose a ball game, they go home, they have a nice dinner, they put their heads down on the pillow and go to sleep. Poor Mel Ott, he can't sleep at night. He wants to win, he's got a job to do for the owner of the ball club. But that doesn't concern the players, they're all getting good money." I said, "You surround yourself with this type of player, they're real nice guys, sure — 'Howarya, Howarya' and you're going to finish down in the cellar with them. Because they think they're giving you one hundred percent on the ball field and they're not. Give me some scratching, diving, hungry ballplayers who come to kill you. Now, Stanky's the nicest gentleman who ever drew breath, but when the bell rings you're his mortal enemy. That's the kind of a guy I want playing for me. That was the context. To explain why Eddie Stanky was so valuable to me by comparing him to a group of far more talented players who were — in fact — in last place. Frankie Graham did write it up that way. In that respect, Graham was the most remarkable reporter I ever met. He would sit there and never take a note, and then you'd pick up the paper and find yourself quoted word for word. But the other writers who picked it up ran two sentences together to make it sound as if I were saying that you couldn't be a decent person and succeed."

Nice guys do not finish last.

Actually, nice guys finish first with a ton of cheerleaders celebrating with you. (Feel free to quote me on that.) Nice gets it done. Nice moves you forward with gusto. Nice keeps you in a place of integrity with yourself. Nice enrolls people to help you accomplish your goals. Nice keeps you moving in the direction of your purpose. Nice smooths the path for yourself. Greases the wheel. Levels the playing field. Keeps you smiling. Picture Pharrell Williams' "Happy" video here. (Okay, if you can't picture it, take a break and go look it up. I'll wait). Can you feel it? That is the feeling being nice can bring. No, it doesn't mean that we spend every day dancing in the aisles with delirious joy. But it can mean that we spend a lot more time with a smile on our face than not. It does mean that the Universe will step up to meet us to help us pursue our dreams.

You do know that the Universe wants you to have your dreams come true, right? It will conspire with you to get them accomplished. There is a universal energy to niceness that permeates the field around you. It is like gravity. (More on that later.)

Watch where people tend to gravitate at any gathering. Chances are it is to the person that is smiling and engaged – not to the guy with his arms crossed and a scowl on his face. Who is going to get the most out of the group? It doesn't matter if it's a party or a workshop. We are all looking for connection and learning.

Nice opens your mind to new information and connections. Not nice does not. (There's a twister of a little sentence now, isn't it?)

Nice leads to success. Successful relationships, successful businesses, success when it comes to your physical well-being, growing in your relationship to God or

Spirit or the Universe or whatever belief system you choose.

Nice moves you forward.

Chapter 3

Nice House Purchase

L et's see what nice can do for you in a real-life situation. How about in a situation that is not necessarily the most stress-free in general and when things can go bad quickly. This is a true story and none of the names have been changed.

Scott and I both are entrepreneurs and have been together for fourteen years. For twelve of those years, we lived in a house we rented that was excellent for our needs and in a wonderful neighborhood. We were comfortable. Right up until we stopped being comfortable. The neighborhood was changing a bit and the house needed some major foundational repairs that were going to require living in a construction zone for six months while they tore out the kitchen and all the flooring; the roof needed to be replaced; and the entire lot regraded. The signs were all there. It was time to make a move and we were ready.

We knew we were coming to the end of our lease and began looking at homes to purchase. We knew what we wanted. The house had to be at least 3,000 square feet, with 5 bedrooms, on an acre or more, allow horses, be near a riding trail, be within the nine square miles of the kid's high-school boundaries and have a shop big enough to build a plane. Those were the specifics ... beyond those criteria, we all had to love it and of course be able to secure the loan to purchase it. To start with, though, there are not that many pockets of horse property within those nine square miles. And of those, there are even fewer that have a structure big enough to build a plane.

We found the perfect house. It met all of our criteria and it had just been reduced from a number we would not have been willing to pay to something within the realm of possibility. It was still a little more than we planned on spending, but according to the mortgage broker we were working with, it was doable. Great! We put a contract on it and proceeded with all the necessary steps. Scott and I have both been self-employed for decades and owned a business together at this point. We have also each had our share of financial challenges along the way. We were assured that with the down payment we had and our business income, we would be approved.

A week or so into the process, the mortgage handler found a nick on our credit report that didn't belong there. To make a long story much shorter, he made a few phone calls to the financial institution that was reporting the bad debt and then told me point blank that not only would we not qualify for that house … there was no way we were going to be able to secure a mortgage – ever! Period … end of story. He took our six-inch pile of documentation and threw it in the shredding bin.

Was I upset? Disappointed? Angry? Yes … all of the above. How did I react? Well, here's the moment where the rubber meets the road. Was I going to remember who I am and what I believe? Was I going to blow a gasket and start screaming like a crazy woman at the unfairness of it all? The problem with the credit report was a mistake! Not even our fault. I would have had every right to go a little nutso. And on top of that I could certainly have decided that the mortgage broker should have noticed that problem long before we were already under contract. He had our credit reports for weeks by then.

Yes … I was upset. Yes, I was frustrated and scared and angry. Yet I reacted with civility. "Thank you for your time; I guess it's time for me to move on." No dramatic exit. No foul language. No tears.

I followed that civil moment with a few minutes of total panic when I reached the safety of my vehicle. What am I gonna do? How am I going to tell Scott this is not going to happen? How disappointed are the kids going to be?

After my panic minute passed, I decided that the best step was to contact our realtor, Shawn, and let him know that we had reached a fork in the road and I needed another mortgage person to see. He was understanding and a little appalled that his number one guy for working on mortgages for the self-employed dropped the ball on all of us. He gave me the name of another person. Stephanie was amazing! Very no-nonsense and business-like. Moves like the wind. Talks even faster. She was the go-getter I needed to get this moving again.

I turned over all the documentation I had from my own files. If you have been through the process, it feels like a personal and professional violation with the amount of information they request. She looked it over, saw the credit-report problem and immediately moved into solution. She told me what I needed to do. I took her advice on who to talk to and what verbiage to use to describe the situation.

To get this worked out, we needed the help and cooperation of bank employees on many levels to get messages and requests through to the attorneys and the credit department that we did not have access to. I am convinced that it was only because the staff I was working with became enrolled in our dilemma that it was able to be resolved. They got enrolled because I treated them really well and with a lot of respect.

I was not assigning blame or using guilt. I was sincerely appreciative of any help they gave me in moving my project forward. I am also certain that if I had approached it with an angry or accusatory tone, the outcome would have been much different. After the problem was removed, one of the managers mentioned that she had never seen the powers that be work so quickly. It was resolved completely in three days. The previous mortgage broker had been attempting to get the same thing done over the course of weeks ... with zero progress toward resolution.

That was one of many roadblocks that we overcame using niceness as my guide.

So now we were on our way! The purchase was back on track and we were moving forward.

The underwriters were very busy doing what underwriters do. I like to believe that they are preventing people from going into more debt than they can handle. That is the nice way to see it. And I must confess there were many times along the way that I felt that they were being very, very picky.

For instance, they were less than excited about the idea that my child-support payment from my children's father was less than what was on the court documents and didn't go through the government agency in charge of tracking such things. I had the documentation that he paid me each and every month, but they didn't like the casualness of the arrangement.

At the time of our divorce, we had already been operating for many years with our own agreement. Those agreements were working just fine and covered decision making, support and time for the children to spend with each of us.

When I got around to filing paperwork to formalize our separation with a divorce, the judge was not thrilled with our agreement. The court calculations for the support he would have to pay were more than double what I had been getting. That amount would have crippled him financially. The judge questioned me fully about whether I knew what I was giving up and questioned how it would help my children to accept less than what the state mandated. I responded that having their dad lose his house didn't seem like a benefit to the children. I didn't see the merit in having him monetarily annihilated and losing his home. That home was the place my small children (at the time) were familiar with and it was in a nice neighborhood.

In the end, she signed off on the divorce decree with all my stipulations intact. I still had the impression that she thought I was a little nuts.

This can be filed under a nice thing to do … or under the heading of selfish. I didn't want to be the cause of Bill having to uproot himself and be in a place where I may not be comfortable when the children were spending time with him. I felt comfortable with them playing outside on their bikes or skateboards in the neighborhood he was in. There is very little traffic and while it is not in a high-end area, the neighbors are all very friendly. Plain and simple, I didn't want the added anxiety and I didn't want to inflict more suffering for anyone.

Anyway, back to our underwriters. They were not happy with our less than formal arrangement. Again, they were going to deny the loan by taking that income off my equation, which threw our debt ratio all out of whack. As Stephanie was explaining this new malfunction, I was feeling a little off balance, but managed to stay calm.

"Okay, so what do we do now?" I asked.

She thought for a while and then started shuffling paper and looking at her monitor as she plugged numbers into her magic mortgage program. What she suggested was that if I pay off a loan I was still carrying on my vehicle with some money from savings, we would have just enough left in the savings account for their 'slush' fund the bank likes to see at closing and removing the loan from my debt column would make the ratio work and I wouldn't have to list the child support as income at all. (I told you she was brilliant, didn't I?)

I ran off to the bank and made that happen immediately. We were off and running again!

The last major hurdle cropped up less than one week from closing. Stephanie called me to meet at her office on Friday afternoon. As I walked around the corner toward her office, I could tell from the look on her face that this was bad. She thought we were done. This was not going to happen.

She proceeded to explain that the underwriters had one more hoop for us to jump through. It appears that the arrangement Scott had with his ex-wife concerning alimony was not enough for them. They had been operating with a verbal agreement for a decade without any problems. What the underwriters needed was a modified alimony order approved and signed by a judge ... and we needed it in 5 business days. Stephanie explained what was needed and said the best we could hope for would be a contract extension because the court process would take 4-6 weeks.

The experience of working with the sellers to that point had clearly shown us there was no way they would hold the house for another month or two.

I was sitting in Stephanie's office and my brain was spinning. This could not be happening! I was feeling a little panicky. But feelings are just feelings ... they do not have to dictate my behavior or way of being.

So I smiled at Stephanie and very calmly said …
"Stephanie, I hear your words and I understand that we have
a problem … AND what can I do now to get this done?" She
looked at me with a strange look as if she didn't know if I
was deaf or just stupid. I repeated my question. Her answer
was "Well, I don't know … unless you know someone that
can write up the legal documents really quickly … get both
Scott and his ex-wife in to get them signed with a notary and
if you happen to know a judge that would sign them by next
Wednesday, we'll be good to go. Other than that, I just don't
know what to tell you."

Well … Scott and I don't have great need of attorneys,
so we didn't exactly have an attorney in our speed dial that
would jump on a moment's notice. Let alone on a Friday
afternoon at 3:00. As it happened, Stephanie's assistant was
overhearing bits and pieces of the conversation from
outside her office. She chimed in with … "What about
those people downtown that write up legal documents, but
they're not attorneys?" Stephanie raised her eyebrows.
Huh? I saw a glimmer of hope. She certainly expressed that
it was a long shot, but I was already on the phone with
them and on my way out the door.

I was at their office within fifteen minutes, explaining
the situation. Again, no whining or gnashing of teeth. No
blame, shame or guilt being tossed around. I let them know

that I really needed their help. I made requests, letting them know that I totally understood that what I was asking was certainly not reasonable and that I would understand if the answer was no. I was not demanding or aggressive. Passionate would be closer. I was, quite simply - nice.

The upshot was that within three hours they had the document ready for signatures. All legal-like with the blue paper behind it and everything! (The little things impress me, what can I say?) They worked with Scott and his ex-wife and met them to notarize their signatures at 8 a.m. on a Sunday morning.

By Monday afternoon, they had secured a judge's signature on the papers and we had them back to the underwriters for processing.

The house closing took place on time and we took possession of the property we wanted.

Again … I have no idea how it would have worked out if they had not been enrolled in my dilemma. And why were they enrolled and willing to help me? Because I believe they liked me and saw my humanity. Again … in a word … I was nice. They were nice. We were all pulling together to reach a goal. In this case, the goal was to move the mortgage process forward, and of course I paid their fees. In addition to that, I have referred more business their way than I can track. Win – win … the power of nice.

Chapter 4

Cake Walks

L ife is not always a cake walk. Does that come as a shock to you? Somehow, I didn't think so. It doesn't matter where you are or what family you were born into … every person on the planet experiences a certain amount of heartache and hardships. It just may not look like it from outer appearances. It is true that we don't know the trials and tribulations of those around us until we have walked a mile in their shoes.

(Who said that? Hang on … I'll go find out. Found it! Steve Martin — 'Before you criticize a man, walk *a mile in his shoes*. That way, when you do criticize him, you'll be a mile away and have his shoes.' Okay, maybe that wasn't exactly the original quote, but you get the picture.)

There are multi-bazillionaires in the world that spend an incredible amount of time and energy worrying about money. They are convinced that at any moment, their fortunes could disappear! Perhaps they would only have a couple of million to live on and recreate their empire!

Other people live on a shoestring and don't give money a second thought. They just know that things will work out.

Some very famous people manage to stay totally grounded in who they are and continue to live their lives enjoying their fame and fortune while using their status to help others. Other celebrities are not quite so stable or magnanimous.

I am sure you have more than a few stories in your memory banks of super-popular celebrities with amazing amounts of talent, plenty of money and looks that defy all reason who are no longer with us because they did not see themselves as valuable enough. They have denied us all the privilege of enjoying their gifts another day. Drug overdoses, whether accidental or intentional, took them out. Why? Any reasonable person would see them as immensely successful. One simple reason comes to mind … they were not nice to themselves.

For the purpose of this book, I would like you to consider that success is much more than money in the bank or a big title on your door or being married with children. Can those things be supremely great to aspire to and to achieve? Absolutely! However, I am sure you, dear reader, are much more mature in your thinking than to believe that those things alone with make you a success. You are infinitely more enlightened than that. How do I know, you ask? Simple … you were brilliant enough to choose this book!

A pleasing personality, or simply being nice, will move you further than you can imagine toward the dream life you picture. It will also produce a much more pleasant journey in the long run. It smooths some of the bumps in the road and creates a life that works on every level.

Are you familiar with *Think and Grow Rich* by Napoleon Hill? No? Oh my goodness … write that down as your very next purchase. It is a tremendous book that will point you in the direction of anything you truly want to attain in this life. It covers much more than being financially rich. If you are familiar with it or you have read his Law of Success, you know that having or developing a pleasing personality is one of his key principles. That is what this book is about – and more.

Chapter 5

Be Nice To Yourself

Nice covers not only how you treat other people, but how you treat yourself as well. Being nice on every level means that you speak kindly to yourself and treat others with respect. You cut yourself a grace card when you are not operating at your peak state of brilliance. Like when you totally mess up and forget to pick up the kale on your way home from the gym.

Oh, I hear your brain flipping out. Buying kale is not even on your radar and going to the gym is not on your schedule right now. It's something you will get around to when a) tomorrow dawns b) the big project is finished at work c) the kids start school d) hell freezes over.

Most people set all kinds of goals for themselves to improve their lives. Maybe for you it's not going to the gym, it's reading for 30 minutes a day or cutting your Facebook time. For some people it's setting a New Year's resolution to lose weight or make more money. We will not always complete all the tasks we give ourselves. Life happens along the way and we adjust as we go. Sometimes we make excuses for our failure to launch, other times it is unexpected circumstances that throw us off the rails; in either case, we can be nice to ourselves without letting ourselves off the hook.

My point is, you can be nice to yourself even when you are not meeting your own preconceived model of how you should be showing up in the world. I look at it this way. I always do my best ... always. I know that about myself. I also happen to believe that my best is on a sliding scale. Today's best may have no resemblance to what yesterday's best looked like.

Some days I am on top of my game and in the flow. Other days it's a struggle to get out of bed in the morning. So, what do I do? Simply practice nice. Does that mean that I allow myself to stay in bed until noon? No ... because that's not really being nice to me. It may feel good in that moment, but in the overall scheme of things ... it's not nice. Why? Because staying in bed doesn't move me forward toward what it is I say I want.

Being nice doesn't necessarily translate into being happy in the short term. It can, but it's not a given. I may be happier by a long shot, staying in my comfy bed dozing happily with a book next to me that I read between twenty minute cat naps.

And let me just say there is absolutely nothing wrong with that scenario. In fact, if that's what you're doing right now, please continue.

Unless, because you are still in bed, you are missing an appointment that will launch your life into the stratosphere and you are planning on using my book as an excuse to sabotage your hopes and dreams. It would not be nice to use this book as a scapegoat.

So back to my definition of nice. Nice, when it relates to you, consists of those actions or thoughts that move you forward. Nice, when considering other people, means tailoring your words and deeds toward helping them move forward as well. And we get the opportunity to practice in the nice zone with other human beings and ourselves at the same time.

Nice means making our journey more pleasant and making the path for other people a little smoother.

When we are smiling and open to what is going on around us, it creates a synergistic energy.

Smiling changes the actual physiology in your brain, because you release more of the good hormones that increase your energy and elevate your mood. Your creative abilities increase as well. When you have a problem, smiling makes it easier to come up with a solution. And you also are more likely to be able to enroll others into helping you resolve the situation. People want to help you. How cool is that?

Nice means everyone moves forward. You and the people around you.

I hear a few of you asking, "Moving forward? What is that? Forward toward what?" Good question! Forward toward new goals. Forward toward improving your relationships. Forward toward finding more inner peace. Forward toward exquisite health. Forward toward your next adventure vacation. Forward toward anything and everything that is important to you. You get to choose where you are going.

This truly is the first day of the rest of your life. If you are not moving forward and growing, you are decaying. Moving forward means staying in hot pursuit of your purpose and your passion. It means being as great as you were meant to be. Great. Magnificent. Extraordinary. Exquisite. Wouldn't it be nice to move into it with grace and a smile?

That's the nicest thing of all. Pursuing your purpose and creating the space to stay in pursuit of that purpose and keeping in mind that everyone has a divine, powerful purpose that deserves to be pursued passionately.

What is your purpose and how does it lead to greatness?

Our purpose is the reason we are here. Each human on this planet has a reason for being here at this very moment in time, and it is divinely inspired. The purpose is different for each of us and each is special beyond all comprehension. We are born with greatness within us and purpose is all about allowing that excellence to manifest in our world. Each purpose on the planet is important and needed. If you want a hint about what your purpose may be, take a look at what you are completely passionate about. What is that you do or dream of doing that takes you out of time and space? When you were a child, what did you dream of doing?

If we each lived our most divine purpose full out without fear, wow! What an amazing world we would create. There will never be another you ... look around you. There will never be another him or her or her or him ... ever! (That little exercise doesn't work quite as well if you are sitting alone in your house reading quietly with your cat on your lap, now does it? Oh well, I have to believe you can imagine looking around and seeing other people or at the very least think of another person that takes up space on this planet. There! That wasn't so hard, was it?)

Living your purpose with passion is the ultimate in nice! Making the choices necessary to keep you moving forward and growing is the greatest action you can take. It doesn't mean that everyone is always going to be totally happy with those choices; and that is a-okay. In fact, it's more than okay, it's perfect. Moving forward is what the Universe wants you to do with your life.

Quiet desperation is a life I am not interested in living. I believe it kills people. Literally. I believe that quiet agony saps the life out of us one painful day at a time … until one day you just stop breathing. There are many ways to make that happen.

Quiet desperation describes a life devoid of joy and challenge. By challenge I do not mean the challenges you face on a daily basis. I'm not talking about the challenge of making ends meet at the end of the month or the challenge of scheduling dentist appointments around the kid's school schedules. I am talking about the challenges where you really take yourself on! You play full out! You do those things that you really want to do and just haven't created the space to do them. This involves taking time to be nice to you.

Choose one thing and see how incredibly alive you feel! It doesn't have to be something you save for months or take a year's sabbatical to attain. It can be as simple as cooking something you have never made before; something new that sounds delicious or something you had in a restaurant and thought you'd love to have again. If you get stuck in the middle of the recipe, there's always YouTube! Perhaps you have always thought that flying a plane would be fun. You'd be surprised at how inexpensive it can be to take a training flight. Save up for it and look forward to the day you have it scheduled! Take an afternoon workshop on painting or gardening. Try what sounds like fun to you!

It doesn't have to be hard … it's simply being nice to yourself.

This "nice" thing is really all about you in the long run. It's about living a life fully on purpose and helping others do the same. Think of it this way: if nice moves you further down the path to fulfilling your actual purpose for being here and it makes the journey more pleasant, why not?

Oh, I hear you whispering under your breath, "Because then I'll be a doormat, that's why."

It most certainly is not!

Nice is a way of being, not a license to be used. Nice means establishing your boundaries and not allowing others to throw you off the rails on the way to your dreams. It could be argued that nice is actually selfish. We won't do that here, of course, because arguing is not nice.

By the way, doormats are only nice when they are sitting outside your front door doing what they were meant to do. They are totally and 100% on purpose, which actually means they are nicer than some people I meet.

But seriously folks, nice does not in any way equate with being a doormat. What is a doormat, anyway? When we refer to other humans as doormats, we often talk about the habit of going along to get along. The doormat's way of being is to never rock the boat, don't disagree, don't voice an opinion, just go along and then people will like them and fill them up with whatever it is they're looking for ... love, validation, acceptance, company, etc. These people give the appearance of being nice, easy-going and friendly. But they are not actually nice, if you use my definition of nice. Nice is any action, thought or language that moves you more deeply toward the ultimate purpose you were put here to fulfill.

Chapter 6

No Doormats Allowed

N ice definitively and absolutely starts with yourself. Being nice to yourself is key. We are not nice to ourselves by putting our needs in second place to someone else's wants and needs although we sometimes tell ourselves that it's the nice thing to do. It's not. It can get a little mucky here, stay with me.

Story time! Follow along, boys and girls ...

You have a friend named Mary. Mary is a lovely girl, who always seems to have a crisis brewing. You're her go-to person for advice and help when she is in trouble. It's always been this way. Mary counts on you to be the responsible one in your relationship. You're always the designated driver.

She expresses tons of admiration for you. She tells you frequently how amazing you are; that you have it all together. In her eyes, you never seem to have any problems at all. It feels great to be you! Go you!

You are on a great trajectory in your life. Things at work are going well. You have been on track with creating real balance in your life. You exercise on a regular basis, eat foods that nourish your body and help you feel like you are in peak performance mode every day. You are having fun with friends and finally have forged a real relationship with your family. It all feels good.

So you are going about your life, excited to be working out daily and staying on course for that promotion you've been after for what seems like forever. Things are going well. No major upheavals. You're within five pounds of being at the weight you've been dreaming about since college! So you're staying on top of all the moving parts of your world when Mary calls with a little problem. Her car seems to be on the fritz again and she could really use a ride to work for a day or two. No problem. You got this. Of course you're gonna help her!

This sounds nice, right? It looks like you are in the nice zone. You are more than capable of making a few minor adjustments to your schedule to help her out of a jam for a couple of days.

And so you jump to the rescue and it's kind of fun to see her first thing in the morning. It takes less than an hour out of your morning and just a little more than an hour in the afternoon, with traffic and all.

That includes the time you spend waiting for her. You don't like being late – ever! So you get to her house a few minutes early. Your friend, however, seems to enjoy the thrill of sliding in at the very last moment. She doesn't really see it as any big deal if she's just a few minutes late. You tell yourself it's not really a problem to wait for her, you can use the time to relax for a few minutes. The ride to drop her off at her workplace is a little more harried than you like because you have to drive a bit aggressively to get her there in time to punch in. But you're used to it.

A few days into this situation the story on the car is changing. It's gonna cost way more than she thought. Now it looks like she won't be able to pick up the car until next payday. You are starting to wonder what you got yourself into – again.

"This is fun, right? It's like we're roomies again!" she tags onto the end of her announcement.

"No problem ..." you reply.

Inside you're thinking that things are getting a little challenging. There were things you needed to get done this week that got sidelined because you are using up two hours a day driving your friend to work and back – plus she had a few errands to run on a couple of nights. The fun is fading. She is also spending most of the trips back and forth on her phone, texting or talking to her new crush. You're beginning to feel more like a cab driver than a hero.

Now that you think about it, it really is like being roommates in college again. Now you remember. It always seemed like she was too busy to help with the basics. Too booked to help clean or take care of food shopping or listen to the challenges going on in your life. Never seemed to have the rent on time or be able to hold down a job.

What's happening here? You agreed to help her out for a few days and now you feel stuck and are getting more irritated by the day. This whole situation is getting really old, really fast. You realize that you are not really breathing very well when she is with you because when she gets out of the car the first thing you do is take a really deep cleansing breath of relief.

What happened to those good feelings from a few days ago? You were happy to help a friend in need. Now you're just aggravated.

Not nice.

Chapter 7
Broken Agreements

H ere's the problem. You dropped out of the nice zone and into the area of doormat. The most common cause of Operation Relocation to Doormatville is broken agreements.

"What agreements were broken here?" you ask. Or maybe on a more basic level, "What is this agreement thing of which you speak?" That would be the question if you suddenly transported yourself into some other dimension of Shakespearian speech patterns.

Agreements are very simply contracts you make with yourself and other humans on the planet. They happen all day, every day. You tell your child you will pick them up at 4 o'clock … that's an agreement. You promise to be faithful to your spouse … agreement. You hire a salesperson and offer to pay them 10% of their sales … agreement. You commit to working out three times a week … agreement with yourself. Got it? Good.

Agreements are the basis of integrity. Keep your agreements to yourself and others and you are living in integrity. Break agreements and you are out of integrity.

Stay out of integrity long enough and you will stop being trusted and stop trusting yourself. That is not nice.

Pop quiz!

What are the Four Agreements according to Don Miguel Ruiz, author of the book of the same name?

Answer:

Be impeccable with your word
Don't take anything personally
Don't make assumptions
Always do your best

What?! You haven't read *The Four Agreements*? Well, stop right here and get that on your list of books to read after this one. Never mind, I'll make you a list at the end of this book with resources that I have found to be immensely helpful. Or you can go to www.thegrowthcompany.net to get a complete and probably never-ending list of fabulous information.

These four agreements are life-changing when implemented into your world! Truly. I wouldn't say it if it weren't true. Why? 'Cause I read the book and do my best to be impeccable with my word. (Get it? Agreements four and one right there ...)

Okay, so let's go back to our saga with Mary. What agreements were broken? It starts with the original conversation. She said she would need a ride for a couple of days while her car was being repaired. You agreed. That's an agreement.

Now we are at the week mark and growing longer. That's a broken agreement. Plain and simple, you agreed to be her private chauffeur for a couple of days. It is getting extended without a new agreement in place.

The agreement could have been renegotiated when things started going awry with her car repair, but it wasn't.

A renegotiation of an agreement is simply creating a new agreement. You get to re-choose your level of involvement based on what will work for you. In this case, it was an assumption on her part that you would just continue to shuttle her around and you didn't correct the notion. At the moment she brought up the delay, there was probably a little warning flare in your gut that signaled danger ahead.

You've felt these? Sometimes it's literally a little flip in your gut, other times it's a foggy feeling in the brain or a voice that screams "Nooooooooooooooooooo!!" Maybe your warning signal is from the old show Lost in Space television show, where a robot flings its arms around and runs in circles saying "Danger, Will Robinson, danger!" If your name is not Will Robinson, that can be a little confusing, or as the robot would say, "Does not compute! Does not compute!"

The point is that we have an internal check valve that will tell us when we are about to jump into doormatville, but we don't always heed the warning. If we did hear it and take action, it would keep us from circumstances like this one where we are feeling used and abused in a relationship we thought we valued.

You also broke an agreement with yourself. You committed to yourself months ago that you were going to create more balance in your life by exercising on a regular basis and making changes to your eating habits that would support a healthier, more energetic you. This new routine would increase your energy and move you forward toward your professional goals as well as being a springboard to launch into a new level of personal confidence. Your thinking is that with your new confidence and of course the new body that goes with those new choices, you're in a much better position to create a relationship that works! Yep … you'll be on the lookout for a new man or new woman to enter your world and you will be ready. You are excited and motivated to stay this course. It's going great! It's not been an easy path, but your routines are supporting you and they are becoming habits.

Those agreements were important to you and you were following through. So what happened? How balanced is your life within this situation with your friend?

While you are practicing being superman, the rest of your world is showing definite signs of neglect. Can you see where you broke that agreement with yourself when you stepped into Doormatville?

Not nice!

Chapter 8

Welcome to Doormatville

L et's review the trapdoor.

A few days into your adventure, you picked your friend up at work so you got home late again. At that point, you realized you hadn't gotten your laundry done, so you stay up two extra hours to get that accomplished and cut your sleep time down to only five hours. Well, it would have been five hours, but Mary also needed a ride in the morning. Now you got less than four hours of sleep. You still make it to work on time, but your brain is a foggy mess of moss and you have that big presentation due tomorrow. So even though you have totally committed to yourself that you are eating healthier and exercising regularly … well… no time for that today. The walk at lunch is certainly not going to happen. You'll be eating at your desk today. But what are you going to eat? The salad place doesn't deliver. But good news! The pizza place does! You'll just eat at your desk … pizza followed by coffee and chocolate from that handy dandy vending machine to keep you moving through the afternoon. No big deal. You'll jump back on the healthy train tomorrow. You tell yourself, "Tonight when I get home, I'll just have a leaf of lettuce for dinner to make up for the million calories I just ingested. Even though I probably burned them all up 'cause I am working so hard on this project that my brain is probably burning a half a million calories a minute not to mention that my fingers are typing sooooooo fast they feel like they are in their own little boot-camp fitness workout. That has to count for something ... right?"

Are you getting the picture? Instead of honoring your agreement with yourself, you are now in damage control and justification.

Broken agreements with ourselves are the most damaging. We literally stop trusting ourselves. It gives the negative voices in our heads power to argue with more conviction than before.

You've experienced this? You decide for the third time to quit smoking or some other habit you know is not serving you, what does your brain immediately say? That's right. It laughs and reminds you that it hasn't worked before, why would it work now? It reminds you of past failures in vivid detail. It brings up feelings of defeat before you even start. If you heard the words your brain uses to stop you in your tracks from anyone else, you could find yourself in a fight. Or you may find that it motivates you. You'll show them! Unfortunately, that kind of argument in your own brain with your very own self is not quite as common. Our self-doubts grab us and we are off the rails.

Not nice!

Chapter 9

Why? Why do we do this to ourselves and each other?

S o why do we set ourselves up for frustration like this? Why do we ignore the warning signs along the way? There are lots of reasons. We think we are being nice. We don't want to upset anyone. We are hoping to qualify for that great eulogy at our memorial service. We just don't like any kind of confrontation. We feel good on the inside when we are helping other people. It raises our self-esteem and our confidence. Do any of these resonate with you?

Most of us like "the juice." The rush. That feeling of being needed.

Admiration … You're such a good person!

Validation … I have never met anyone as selfless as you are!

Promotion … telling anyone they meet what an incredible cook, friend, driver, typist, etc. that you are. Perhaps you are the best grass-mower in the whole country!

That feeling of being needed is heady stuff. You can puff up your chest just a little as you go through your day.

A little bit of a Superman complex comes bleeding through.

The duration between "Yes! I am Superman. Thank you." And "What have I gotten myself into?" varies. It can be moments or days or weeks or even years, depending on the situation and the people involved. No matter when it rears its head, you can count on the fact that you have absolutely stepped out of the nice zone.

Now let's take a look at her side of the equation. Where is Mary on the "nice" scale?

She knows you're her friend and that you truly care about her and the rough stretch of highway she's found herself on. She also thinks she's being nice. She expresses a ton of gratitude for your help in getting her where she needs to be. She doesn't see herself as being this needy, but when her husband left, her boss cut her hours in half and the car broke down, she was beside herself! And there you were! Her own personal super hero. She knew she could count on you to help her through. She tells everyone how wonderful you are and how she wouldn't know what she'd do without you in her corner. You're totally amazing!

She looks to you as an example. Your life is always so perfect. You have it all. The perfect job, the perfect home, great relationships with your family. Nothing really every goes badly in your world. You're so lucky! Even when bad things happen, you rise to the top of the heap and move on. You never complain about money or time or really anything at all. You're always on an even keel.

She knows you are going out of your way a little, but she also believes that you are enjoying your time with her. You have always seemed kind of serious. In fact, she sees your life as actually pretty boring, so she spices things up with a little drama from her world. This is how your friendship has always been. This little situation should be over soon and then she'll make it up to you somehow. Buy you a drink at the next happy hour. She knows you don't usually go to happy hours, but she's sure she can talk you into it.

In her mind, this is status quo because you have her trained well.

Did you know we do that? Train other people how to be in our world? We do. We let people know exactly how much or in some cases how little we expect from them. In this case, she has come to expect that you will be there for her anytime she calls and all she needs to bring to the table is her drama. She likes having you around. You help her shine. She's very comfortable with the way things are.

After all, you have it all and she is struggling all the time. True, there might be a little piece deep inside her that may actually resent you just a little. Bringing a little upheaval into your world is good for you. It evens the imaginary score in some way.

You know that feeling? You notice a woman who appears to have it all together. She's beyond attractive. And immediately there is a little voice in your head that says "I don't like her!" She hasn't even opened her mouth and you already dislike her intensely. Or perhaps you're at a party and there is a guy who has a tight circle of people around him laughing as he tells story after story of his adventures in Patagonia and his life as an international soccer star. All you want to do as you watch him is somehow knock him off the pedestal he's created for himself.

This feeling of competition is what contributes to our tendency to stop each other like crabs in a bucket. You know about this, right? If you throw one crab in a bucket, the first thing it will do is attempt to escape by reaching for the rim of the container. If you throw another crab in and it attempts escape, the first one will pull it back into the bucket trying to pull itself out. No one wins.

There is no need for comparison or competition. We all live in an abundant and full universe, full of options and ideas. There is no need to compete or step on the next guy's gifts. You have your own to pursue and develop. No need to look over your shoulder for judgment. We are all perfect AND all flawed in our own unique and beautiful ways.

Beauty is within us all. There are those who say that he or she is better than me … this is not a true statement. There is no better. You are the absolute perfect you, never to be duplicated.

It is the competition that kills the passion within and stops people from fulfilling their divinest purpose in life.

Not nice.

Chapter 10

Ugh

Back to the story: while the car saga is going on in the background of Mary's life, she meets this new guy. They have had only a few dates, but she really, really likes him! It's so exciting after being with her husband who didn't appreciate her. Now someone is interested in every word she says! And he thinks she's sexy too! This is heady stuff! He wants to whisk her away for a weekend on the beach in the Bahamas. It's just three days, but wow, she hasn't felt this excited in years. She's had a rough go lately and really feels like she deserves this weekend away. He says he's going to pay for everything … she would just want to take a few hundred bucks to maybe buy some meals and miscellaneous things along the way … like maybe a parasailing adventure. Ooooooo … that sounds like fun! She wouldn't want him to think she is using him. She'd only have to take off a couple of days of work. Counting the money she would spend and the money she wouldn't earn, the cost would only set her back a week or so in getting her car back on the road again. She knows you'll understand.

Are you catching the gist of where this is going? You've been burning the candle at both ends to help her out of her dilemma and now she's treating herself to a little getaway with her new man while you will spend that weekend catching up with all the work and personal things that have been pushed to the side while you cart her around to work and shopping and just generally making sure she is taken care of.

This is where some of the irritation is spawning wings. You are feeling used and abused. The Superman warm fuzzies are growing cold and prickly. When she calls, you are feeling irritated and annoyed. You get just a little bit aggravated listening to her talk about her new man. Actually, "snarky" kind of sums it up. This is not feeling like fun anymore. Now it's just work.

You want to be happy for your friend, but somehow it's just not working for you. You do your best to sound excited about her new adventure, but mostly you are tired and worn out. Even when she remembers to ask how you're doing, you feel sharp and irritated. You don't want to burst her bubble by telling her how you really feel.

I mean really feel.

"Well, Mary, I am kind of doing okay. Other than the fact that I have had like two hours of sleep every night for the past week because of hauling you all over town ...

getting you to work, doing your errands and not to mention the extra shopping trip so you could buy some new lingerie for your trip. Then I make up the time I am spending with you by working into the wee hours of the morning so I don't fall any more behind at work.

"My sister thinks I have lost my ever-lovin' mind. I actually skipped my niece's choir concert because I had to get on the phone with a client to make up for the early-morning meeting I missed while I was getting you to work again!

"Not to mention that I have had some problems, too. The washer died and the repairman declared it dead. Who has time to go shopping for a new one? And the laundromat takes forever! Good thing they're open late and I can bring my laptop and get some work done.

"I also just realized that my bank account is getting dangerously low. I just figured out I am spending a fortune on food these past few weeks. Why, you ask? Because I haven't been cooking. I've been picking up fast food almost every night. I have been ordering food every day to eat at my desk, too. That costs tons more than when I pack my own to eat at the park during my lunch break. Oh, and I feel like poop without my daily walk. But where can I grab the thirty minutes to do that?

"And in the meantime I get to hear how excited you are to be going away for the weekend with your new Mr. Perfect with the chiseled nose and a perfect six-pack who speaks fourteen languages and has more money than Warren Buffet and he opens every door for you and tells you how beautiful you are every hour on the hour.

"Yeah ... I'm fine. It feels like I am on a hamster wheel with no sign of relief in sight. In a way I am looking forward to you being gone for a few days so I can get a break from both your whining over money and your car and your gloating over your new crush and the trip to the Bahamas. I'll be hoping you find a job on the island and just stay there! Other than that ... life is just peachy! Have a nice day."

You may be wondering ... what happened to nice here? Where did it go from nice to help a friend in need to "OMG, get that woman away from me!"

Just to be clear, when you are harboring feelings of anger and resentment, you are not sitting pretty in the nice zone, even if you are doing your best not to put your anger on display. That smile on your face doesn't negate the power of the negative emotion boiling in your belly.

So did your help serve her? You were being nice, right? I'm gonna say that based on my criteria of moving people forward toward their purpose as being nice … no, this wasn't nice.

It did actually help her … stay stuck.

Not nice.

Chapter 11

True Nice In Action

Y our 'help' reinforced the belief that Mary is helpless and incapable. Nice is holding people capable and accountable. This is not always welcomed or even especially pleasant, but it's the nice thing to do. So what would nice have looked like when a friend needs assistance? Do we throw up our hands and say, "Wow, too bad, so sad?" Don't we ever get to jump into our hero costume and save the day?

Of course we do! There will always be opportunities to don that cape and rush in on a high of adrenaline. The point is to choose those moments consciously and make sure you are actually being nice. Nice enough to actually assist in helping people move forward and not stay stuck.

What might that have looked like in the situation with Mary?

Nice could look like supporting her by working on options together; by sitting down and developing an action plan to help her become more self-sustaining. Maybe you look at the public transportation schedules and routes together to see what would work. Maybe take those routes with her the first time or two to help her feel more secure that she can do this. Maybe you brainstorm ways for her to create more money in her world. You may help her schedule an appointment with an attorney to see if she might be entitled to some financial support from her soon to be ex-husband even before the divorce is filed. Perhaps she can force the sale of his huge collection of Playboy magazines?

You may be just the validating source she needs to show her that she is smart, resourceful and creative. You are not the only one who can handle problems.

It's an amazing thing to behold what happens when you create and hold the space for someone to step up. Even the simplest question can open the opportunity. "Wow, so what are you gonna do now?" is super powerful! As long as you can resist the urge to give them your answers immediately! Even if their answer is I don't know … if you stay with it … they do know. Trust that people have their own answers. Their answers may not be your answers, and that's okay. They don't have to be. They will figure it out. Let them. Hold them capable. Even the most desperate people in the most dire straits will find solutions. Believe in them enough to let them. That is nice at its most brilliant! If your friend thinks it's a good idea to sell her couch to finance her trip to the Bahamas ... great! It may not be your first choice ... and it doesn't need to be. Again, she will figure it out.

Before you go thinking this makes you a mean person because you didn't martyr yourself taking on the problems of others, please back up and actually consider your friend and the power she will feel as she works herself out of the crisis and onto solid ground without using you as a crutch. There is no power in victim-mode. It creates only more victim-ness and resentment of not only you, but anyone else who has more than she does ... more money, more options, better-looking feet, a stable family, whatever. Giving her a taste of the power to create her own life ... a life that works ... THAT is nice!

The scenario of you doing everything for her is not nice – not only does it turn you into a doormat; it reinforces her belief that she is incapable of handling her own life. It leaves everyone feeling dirty.

Not nice.

Chapter 12

Nice and Easy – Children

The easiest way to explain what I've been talking about is to think of children. How often do we tell ourselves that it is just easier to do something ourselves than watch a child struggle through the challenge? For instance, dinner is complete and the dirty dishes are calling for some attention. Is it easier to just go do it yourself or watch your ten-year-old diddle around with them for an hour? He has no rhythm, no system and seems to have forgotten all the steps you have shown him ten times. Is it frustrating to watch? Yes, it can be. Can he get it accomplished? Yes, eventually. Is it possible you are going to rewash a few pots tomorrow? Again, yes. Would he think it super nice if you did it yourself? Yes, yes he would! Is that the nice thing to do? Uhh, no, no it's not.

In the grand scheme of things, it is much nicer to give him the experience of getting something challenging accomplished than to relieve him of the challenge as soon as things look difficult.

If you consistently jump in and save children from ever feeling the pressure of challenges followed by the sense of accomplishment that comes with completion, you are hobbling them. They will come to believe they are not capable of figuring things out and overcoming difficult circumstances. Not nice.

There was a teacher at the Montessori school my children attended through the sixth grade. Their program was set up that a child would have the same teacher for three years. So the first, second and third grade were in one class and the fourth, fifth and sixth were together in another. Each of my three children was assigned in succession to a teacher named Cassi for their fourth through sixth grade years. She is one of the most gifted educators I have ever experienced and also one of the most powerful.

I can honestly say that she had a huge influence on my children, but also on me as a parent. There were rules for the parents of her students. At the beginning of the year she sent home contracts (agreements) that set up everyone's roles for the year. There were rules of conduct covering all the bases. Contracts that cover not only homework expectations for the students, but what is expected from parents if a child doesn't do his or her work or what to do if your child forgets to bring something to school – such as homework or lunch.

If a child forgot to bring lunch, the expectation was that the child would simply not have a lunch that day. A parent was not to jump on their white horse and rescue the child. We would have to trust that they would survive the day and learn from the experience. The first time it happened I went a little crazy on the inside, first beating myself up. "I knew I should have made sure it was sitting by his binder!" Worrying about my little bunchkin most of the day. "I'm sure he's starving! His stomach is probably cramping up by now. He may not survive! He's probably crying in a corner by himself. He's gonna be scarred for life! Maybe I can bake a saw in a cake and he can make a break for it and meet me at the car for his Batman lunch box!" My internal dialogue is not always completely brilliant or rational.

The funny thing was that when I picked him up in the afternoon, he didn't even mention the torturous day he had experienced. When I brought it up, he was as nonchalant as you can possibly imagine. "Oh yeah ... that's right. I forgot my lunch this morning. I was scared I was going to get in trouble, but it turned out to be no big deal. My friends gave me some of theirs and Cassi had some extra crackers and cheese from the open house." It was hardly a conversation that showed any sign of permanent damage.

I would kid with other parents that having a child in Cassi's class is like being schooled yourself. That first year was interesting as I got my mind around the idea that Cassi was setting the pace when it came to my children and their experience in school. Her expectations extended outside the classroom as well. Her influence was felt throughout the family from day one. She expected the very best and she got it.

She uses *The Four Agreements* as a base and builds from there. She is not kidding when she tells incoming families they can expect to work hard and play even harder. Agreements and communication are paramount to having the best experience in her class. And as you work within the parameters she sets, you realize that it works outside her class just as effectively.

She set the children up to win on every level and always held them completely capable of being responsible for themselves and each other. She provided a backdrop of love and support while never buying in to their dramas. They were encouraged to bring any kind of problem to her for guidance and yet she would never give them the answer. It was always a process of exploring possible solutions with kindness and clarity.

The children in her classes learn quickly that their choices will determine their experience. Every time without fail. Through the eight years of experiencing Cassi's mode of teaching and loving my children, I can honestly say she made me a better parent.

Nice!

Chapter 13
Choices and Results

That exceptional teacher was an absolute master at allowing her students to understand that there were natural outcomes to the choices they were making. To master that concept at a very young age is phenomenal. It's a building block that some adults are missing.

Which reminds me, add another book to the list. If *How To's Were Enough We'd All Be Skinny, Rich and Happy* by Brian Klemmer. Brian Klemmer was a leader and a teacher. He founded a company called Klemmer & Associates to help people find their own brilliance and let go of their limiting beliefs. He was fond of reminding people that every moment is a choice and every choice has prices and benefits. Choice is the key. When you realize you are at choice every moment of every day, you have all the power you need to move yourself anywhere you say you want to be.

The programs he set up are literally life changing. His philosophies are incredible for building self-awareness and developing ways of being that will continue to support you to great heights. Much of who I am today, I credit to the work I have done with Klemmer and Associates. His experiential learning is aimed at exposing those areas of your life that are keeping you stuck. How you show up in the world is shown to you in vivid color.

Much of Brian's teachings are shared throughout this book, as they are totally ingrained into my belief system – and they work. Another of my favorite Brian Klemmer-isms is that he based everything on results. As he would evaluate a program or check the accountability of some action, he would say, "Based on results, often harsh, always fair." And then he would move into feedback. There was no gray area for Brian. Either you got the results you were looking to achieve or you didn't. Period.

He stayed in the nice zone. He moved people forward like, no kidding! And he continues to do so through his company and the exceptional facilitators he trained. He passed away suddenly in 2011, so we no longer have the privilege of being in his physical space. I am forever grateful that his vision and his plans extended long past his physical passing. Leaving his legacy to carry on past his life time was nice.

When we look outside of ourselves for the cause of the results we are creating, we have given up all power to make changes. When we believe something was done to us, we stop believing in the possibilities of creating change in our lives. This is playing the victim.

When we allow others to play victim, we hobble them. Seeing other humans as capable is the nicest thing you can do for them. It is much more valuable than simply doing things for them. Freedom is the greatest gift – freedom from dependency on you or anyone else. Fostering and nurturing the belief that they are totally capable of making good choices and moving themselves forward is a huge gift.

Being available to your friends is a nice thing when they could use some additional support to move forward. Making all their decisions for them or doing all the heavy lifting to make their lives comfortable is not nice. It's an ego-driven endeavor to make you feel better. It is rooted in your own belief that somehow you are going to make yourself look good. And you need to make yourself look good because at some deep level you believe you are not good enough just the way you are. Counterintuitive? Probably. That doesn't make it any less true.

This doesn't mean that charitable acts are wrong on any level. Doing things for others with no concern of payback or validation is wonderful. Providing food to those who are homeless feels really, really great. Packing goodies for children who have nothing to call their own is wonderful. Anonymously buying lunch for a random couple who look like they are having a rough day is totally awesome. Do those things just for the fun of it! My challenge is to recognize that even the most altruistic acts are driven by an internal selfish streak. We want to feel good about ourselves and the contribution we are making to the world. Whether you are planting a tree or serving the homeless community nutritious food or giving oodles of cash to rebuild a neighborhood youth center, you are getting juiced. We are wired to feel good when we help others. It's a classic win-win. Let's not pretend that we are selfless when we choose to do those charitable acts. We are still getting a payoff. The emotional juice is priceless. It raises our self-esteem and keeps us moving.

We are all part of this world and have great influence on one another. Being in contribution to each other is a very powerful tool.

My theory is that if we support each other in ways that count, we can all be part of moving the world forward in significant ways.

We live in a very abundant universe. There is more than enough of everything that matters. We may have a difficult time seeing it at this time, but the world is full of possibilities and solutions for even what appears to be impossible challenges. The human spirit and human ingenuity is infinite.

I truly believe that if even a small percentage of the humans on the planet stepped into their true brilliance in pursuit of their passion, the world would change.

What's required to get that accomplished? It's very simple. Notice, I didn't say it's necessarily easy. Simply get out of your own way and help others do the same. Yes, this boils down to nice.

The internal programs that we run with ourselves that stop us from being everything we are capable of being are exactly what creates those lives of quiet desperation. That is not a good place to create the world you want for yourself or the rest of humanity either.

The feelings of inadequacy are crippling not only individuals on the planet, but the whole planet itself. The answers to all of our pressing problems are out there waiting to be discovered and implemented. The only way to get that done is to get out of our own way.

First place to start is by being nice to yourself. Creating clarity from within that you are responsible for your results. You are the one in charge of how your life plays out. You are the one that has the power to change.

There are programs out there to assist you. I personally utilize not only decades of study in the realm of personal development, but Neuro Linguistic Programming to get my clients moving forward and clear to make choices that work.

Allow yourself to fully claim the gifts you were given and move.

Being nice is certainly part of the equation.

Chapter 14

Theological Mapping

O h … I still haven't shared my overall philosophy … are you ready now? Here it is … be nice.

No, I wasn't asking you to be nice by not judging my theological musings. I am saying that encompasses my theological musings: Be nice. That's it in a nutshell. That covers all of it – the Ten Commandments and The Golden Rule, all rolled in. My belief is that there are similar dictates in every spiritual practice. Not lying or stealing or hurting others is as basic a law as there is. And that in a nutshell is in these two little words:

Be – as in step into your being-ness, stay in the present moment, seize the day, etc.

Nice – stay open, kind, courteous, brilliant and allow the universe to supply you with all that you need to meet the big purpose you were meant to bring into this world and help others do the same.

When you are in a place of nice, it is not possible to steal, lie, covet or do harm or any of the other things we know are not in alignment with your own highest good. It is the ultimate in treating others as you'd like to be treated.

So there it is ... my one-stop-shop for all decisions and choices: Is it nice?

Let's think about this for a moment ... who are we the least nice to in our daily lives? It's usually the person we spend the most time with. And who is that? Yourself! Just listen to yourself sometime. We would certainly hear ourselves clearly if we repeated those internal conversations out loud. How many times a day do you think negatively about you?

When you make a mistake, do you automatically beat yourself up? You know, those little comments you make under your breath. Or the sigh and the thought that runs in your mind, "I'm so clumsy!" or "How many times am I going to do that before I learn?" or "I knew I wouldn't get that answer right. I should've kept my mouth shut!" or "Dagnabit!" (That last one is for my readers that don't say "Dammit!")

This is not nice at all. It doesn't move you forward or get you any closer to fulfilling your purpose on this planet. So stop it!

Nice means always using other people's basic goodness as a default. Believe that people are inherently good and go from there. Remember that everyone comes into this world with a divine purpose. It is the basic way of being. So treating all people by first remembering their innocence makes it a lot easier to bring on the niceness.

Seeing the innocence is easy when you try. This goes for you, as well. You were born innocent, too. All we can do is our best … and our best is a variable. Some days we are ready to move through the daily minutiae with grace and ease. We are patient with our children, organized and motivated to tackle the challenges of the day in complete peace. Other days? Not so much. There may be clues as to why some days just flow better than others. Are we getting enough sleep? Perhaps getting to bed at 3 a.m. when your alarm is set for 6 a.m. is not the most conducive way to experience a day of grace. What in the world are we eating? A steady diet of marshmallows and caramel corn may not be what your body needs to keep all the parts operating at peak performance. What kind of self-nurturing do you allow yourself? Do you have days so packed there is no time to breathe? Do you feel you can't take two minutes to breathe deeply without falling behind the curve? Where does exercise fit in the equation?

Taking care of ourselves on every level is nice. When you keep your tank full you are going to be much more inclined to keep moving forward. Balance is a key component to living a life that works.

Taking your mission to "obsession" level is pretty common and actually applauded in some arenas. I think there is value in going to extremes for short periods of time. It creates excitement and flow when you are completely consumed by a project or goal. And it is important to remember that we have many facets to our lives. Being obsessed in one area can throw the whole wheel out of balance and hobble us. Hobbling ourselves is not nice.

This is where the unhappy multi-bazillionaire or the uber-successful comedian who is also a drug addict comes in. Or think about the moms in your life. Are they living lives of quiet desperation because they do not create time to nurture themselves? How about the dads? Are they skipping time with their children because they are working 60-plus hours a week?

Their lives are not in balance. They are focused only on one piece of the pie and the rest is getting soggy and stale. This is again … not nice.

Remember that we have to be on top of our own list of people we are nice to. Only then can we actually be sincerely nice to other people. No … seriously, if you haven't mastered being nice to yourself on a consistent basis, there is no way you can be genuinely nice to others.

Again, be nice to yourself and nice to others and the Universe does cartwheels to support your dreams and desires. It is wired that way.

Be nice to everyone, including you.

Chapter 15

True Purpose

"I'm gonna be a prima ballerina!"

"I'm gonna be an astronaut and build a house on Mars!"

"Oh yeah? Well, I'm gonna be President of the United States!"

"When I grow up, I'm feeding all those starving children in India so I don't have to eat my broccoli!"

And the list goes on. I don't remember ever hearing a child say anything about living paycheck to paycheck or becoming addicted to crack. As small children, we were not stopped by limited thinking. We knew it was all in our grasp and we were excited to grab it and go. Along the way there came all kinds of calls to be reasonable or who did we think we were? Perhaps what you heard was, "What? You think you're so special that you should be rich and famous?" (Read that last one with a thick New York accent; being a Long Island girl, that's what I heard.) We may have been ridiculed if we shared our deepest dreams with other people.

I am not a religious person. I am a spiritual person. I often use the term Universe. I use it all the time in reference to what can be called universal energy, God, Source, the great infinite, whatever name you use to refer to as the source of all things. I believe in an energy source that actually had a hand in creating this world and the universe at large including planets and stars. To infinity and beyond! Maybe I should change my verbiage to the Great Infinite instead of Universe?

Anyway, back to what I was actually getting at … when I refer to Universe I am talking about the energy source and the accompanying energy that it created. I may say things like the Universe wants you to have all that you dream of having and be all that you dream of being. The Universe is geared to meet you and grant you all your wishes when your true intention is lined up cleanly and you begin to take action in the direction of your passion and dreams. I do not have a picture of some grandfather-type figure head who is concerned with my daily challenges and victories. I have trouble picturing any figure, god-like or not, really all that caught up in my daily minutiae. I am more of the mindset that the Universe or God in the original plan set up an energy that works that way. Call it the Law of Attraction or Karma. I believe that it was set in place for our benefit, much in the same way that gravity was put in place for us. It's pretty convenient to have things kind of "glued" down as we go through our daily lives, don't you think?

Well, the Universe has a system in place so that when we are clean and clear and moving in the direction of our purpose, it meets us and supports us with circumstances and people placed on our path to guide us along and help us meet those goals.

Those "coincidences" happen spontaneously ... I don't believe they are accidental. I believe they are being orchestrated on our behalf. It is like there is a magnetic field that pulls those people and circumstances into our field of vision to help us along the way. It is a beautiful thing to behold when it is all in alignment.

Ideas will often pop spontaneously from your unconscious brain into your consciousness when you are clean and clear on what it is you want. Brian Klemmer called this phenomenon the Formula of Champions. He put it in formula form: "intention + mechanism = result." Napoleon Hill said, "Whatever the mind of man can conceive and believe, it can achieve." These both address the same thing.

The secret is to believe.

Remember our crabs in the pot example. We must stop thinking there is not enough for everyone to flourish.

The message is that there is no need for comparison or competition. We all live in an abundant and full universe, full of options and ideas. You have your own to pursue and develop. No need to look over your shoulder for judgment. Beauty is within us all. There are those who say that he or she is better than me … this is not a true statement. There is no such thing as better. You are absolutely the very most perfect you on the planet. It is the competition that literally kills the passion within and stops people from fulfilling their divinest (is that a word?) purpose in life.

There are so many people on the planet who have totally forgotten the big bold dreams they had as small children.

The passion that was placed within you was meant to be realized on every level, as it would not have been placed in your heart if it was not meant to be realized. Very simply, it is your purpose. Do not be confused. Your true purpose can be multi-faceted when it comes to putting it into action. The original that you may remember from childhood as "I want to be a ……" may not match fully your true purpose for being on the planet. For instance, if your original desire was to be a prima ballerina but your body looks more like the profile of a Playboy Bunny, well, short of massive surgery, the chance of dancing the lead at the Met is pretty slim. Does that mean your passion was wrong? Obviously your physicality doesn't match the vision statement. But what if what you really felt that you initially translated into "I want to be a prima ballerina" was really more like this …

"I want to move people's hearts through dance in a way that lights them up on all levels?"

What if in your child-mind the only match you saw for that was dancers on stage and the prima ballerina had the most effect on your soul? What if you didn't have the vocabulary or the understanding to express that? So what you decided as a small child was that being a prima ballerina was your purpose.

Here's the thing - it's the feeling beneath the focus that points to your unique purpose. Not the act ... not the career itself.

Your purpose is not your career. For example, I have been living my purpose for decades. I just didn't find the exact, right fit of a career until a few years ago. I lose all track of time and space when I am coaching someone to overcome the obstacles to getting to their best life yet. I am completely at peace and excited when I am teaching or speaking to audiences. I felt the same way and did the same thing whether I was managing a restaurant or designing closet systems or conducting training meetings.

When I was in sales positions it was the same thing. I was there to help the customer solve a problem any way I could – even if it meant I sent them elsewhere. I am fully in my purpose when I am supporting people in moving forward.

My purpose is to allow and nourish others to break free from their cocoons, spread their wings and fly.

This translates throughout everything I do. Parenting, or working, or volunteering opportunities. Your true purpose works the same way.

Nice.

Chapter 16

Millionaire Dreams

When someone says, "I want to be a millionaire!" what are they actually saying? Do they really believe that having seven figures in their bank account is going to make a difference to their soul? I don't believe it does.

Yes … I hear you screaming a million dollars would be fantastic! THEN I'd be happy! I would still argue that the million dollars has nothing to do with it. It's what the million DOES that makes the real difference in your equation. Having a million dollars opens lots of possibilities. And it still, in and of itself, does not fulfill your passionate purpose.

The person who really, really wants those millions also has a purpose in their life. But it's something bigger than having a million in the bank. What could that be? Could it be that they really want to make a difference? Most likely if that were the case you would hear it immediately after the "I want a million dollars" statement. When I have a million dollars I will (insert good works here).

If you haven't heard those dots line up as they spoke their goal, I don't believe it's likely they will achieve it. There is most likely something deeper. We could say they want to win or are looking for validation or acceptance, but again those are not pointing to their internal passion implanted long ago … before they were born. One way to dig it out would be to keep asking what they would do with their time if they achieved their goal. The result of someone actually amassing large sums of money but not pursuing their passion usually ends up with them setting a new higher goal or losing it all.

Having more money is great. More money to explore possibilities is wonderful. Traveling to different places allows us to have a deeper understanding of other people on the planet and where they come from and how they live and think. It's marvelous for your growth. Money allows for the possibility of making a real difference in other people's lives. You have the chance to provide a hand up or jobs to lift others up into a different financial place. You can also create real change for groups of people. Fresh water or schools in places that don't have the resources. Food or medicine to aid children. Homes for veterans that have been displaced and forgotten along the way. There are so many worthy and worthwhile causes in the world.

Jana Stanfield wrote a great song that says, "I cannot do all the good that the world needs, but the world needs all the good I can do." She is a motivational songstress whose message is amazing. If you ever have the opportunity to hear her speak and perform … do it.

So how do we dig out our truest deepest purpose? It will take some detective work. It doesn't have to be a chore; it can be fun. You'll know you have arrived when you see and feel the energy shift to a deeper place. Does that make sense? The change will be palpable and real. There is an energy of excitement around the discovery.

So what can that look like? It's a matter of digging deep into those things that used to bring you joy. Those things you used to do when you would totally lose track of time. Things you would do even if there was no money involved.

As I mentioned, people's passions and dreams often are squashed early on. There is a good chance that happened before the age of five. So where to go to renew those passions and dreams? And why exactly should we bother? Why isn't it enough that we are driven to achieve? Well … it is and it isn't. Achieving your goals and having things are great! And there has to be something more – something to light hearts on fire to fulfill the highest vision. We can be a rather consumptive society, filled with goals that lead to more goals. If money is the sole goal … there will never be real satisfaction; always a sense of needing more. There is no real end to that game.

There will always be a bigger, better, faster car; a bigger, better home with a better view; a larger portfolio to be attained. When does it end? It's a rat-on-a-wheel sport. Advertisers count on it. Sexier. Handsomer. Better. My point is NOT that goals and acquisitions are bad, it's that acquisition for acquisitions' sake is empty.

What are you doing that totally lights you up? Where do you get to joyful? The enjoyment must last more than the immediate rush of the goal completed/the purchase made. A place of full gratitude. And more than that, too. More than gratitude? How can that be? There is no higher place, they say. Who are "they" anyway? They are probably right – and perhaps that's open to interpretation as well.

Did you ever meet someone who was in such a self-proclaimed state of gratitude that they stopped moving forward? You've met them. "I'm not interested in money, I have everything I need." "I don't really want a relationship … I'm happy with my own company." "I didn't really want that promotion, who needs the pressure?"

This is complacency and it is selfish. Yes, I said it. Selfish.

If all you are concerned about is your own comfort and needs you are sitting in a lonely and self-destructive space.

I used to think that being satisfied where I was with what I had was a dangerous place to be. I thought that staying unhappy and unsatisfied would keep me moving forward. Being okay where I was converted itself in my mind to being complacent. I thought that was the kiss of death as far as making my dreams of success reality.

Through repeated work with Klemmer and Associates and hearing the message from different facilitators, I finally got the message. Satisfaction does not equal complacency. I am totally capable of being satisfied WHILE I strive for more, better and different in different areas of my life. I am always looking for improvement; moving my relationship with my children from a solid seven/eight to a ten on a scale of one to ten; being super grateful for the home I live in and looking to add even more pleasure to it with some renovations or paint or perhaps a pool; still loving the SUV I drive and starting to wonder what I would like as my next vehicle; loving my coaching business and adding value with more training and touching more people with workshops and webinars and this book and speaking engagements. You get the picture?

Being satisfied just means that I live in a place of gratitude while I keep moving forward into an even higher vision for myself.

This life is an adventure and we are meant to grow. Grow into our dreams. Always. Day after day and month after month and year after year. It is not about never being satisfied. It's about always being excited for what now, what next? What else can I learn? What else can I explore? What do I want to do now to grow myself?

So there is a passion within that must be fulfilled in order to truly live this life we chose. The reason to pursue the passion is to make sure that the legacy we leave is the fullest possible and that we enjoy the ride.

That's nice!

Chapter 17

How to Stay in the Nice Zone

Things aren't always smooth in life, so how do you stay nice when things are less than ideal? That's a really good question. The simple answer is that you choose to. Simple doesn't mean easy.

My mom taught me early that when things get crazy, you get creative. I refer to the technique as "tell yourself another story." It takes some imagination, and it can be really fun when you get the hang of it.

Allow me to set the stage for the drama that gave me this incredibly valuable tool.

We have to start in a nice, middle-class neighborhood on Long Island with a stay-at-home mom and a working dad, two older brothers and me. Dad has a good job and mom takes care of us full time. There's a swing set in the back yard and a pool, too. I'm six years old; my brothers are eight and eleven. We look like the ideal family ... from the outside. Inside tells a different story. I know there are a lot of stories that start this way. Brings me a certain sadness to know that it is a common saga.

Most people see Dad as a responsible family man. We attend church services three times a week as a family. He always works hard and makes a good living. He is well liked and respected at his company. Dad is also a functional alcoholic.

The fact was that he really liked to drink. Frequently and heavily. He was not a happy drunk. He was a raging drunk. He would go out after work and have a few. And by a few, I mean a few too many. When he would roll in sometime in the middle of the night, he'd be looking for a fight. This would happen after my brothers and I were in bed for the night. The fights were horrific to hear. Things breaking and lots of screaming. Dad's voice bellowing up the stairs. We could hear mom's voice, but it was softer. It seemed like she was always trying to calm him down.

Mom didn't realize that my brothers and I were fully aware of the fighting going on in the middle of the night. I guess she must have thought we slept through the crashing objects being thrown or the sound a fist makes going through a door.

On a few occasions, my mother would come and get us in the middle of the night after my father passed out. She'd pack us into the car to go to her parents' house. A day or two at grandma's house would pass and then dad would show up all smiles for us and apologies for mom and we would pack up again and go home until the next episode.

After a couple of these incidents, my oldest brother began telling me and my brother that it would be a good idea if we slept with our clothes on if dad wasn't home when we went to bed. He figured it would be safer and faster for us to get out of the house if we were already dressed and had a bag packed.

It happened a few times without major glitches. Mom would wake us up, load us in the car … and off to grandma's we would go. It wasn't a very long trip.

One particular night, dad was raging; then was quiet. Mom woke us up quietly and ushered us to the car, only to find that the car wouldn't start. Mom wasn't really mechanical, but just in case it was something obvious, she popped the hood. Well, it was obvious, all right. Obvious that Dad had disconnected a bunch of wires. I guess he thought he had figured out the rules of engagement in fighting with mom. He must have thought that if the car was incapacitated, then Mom couldn't leave. Well, he underestimated her.

After studying the situation for a few minutes, Mom couldn't figure out how to get that car started. She was also not going to give up on the idea that she was leaving and taking us with her. Mom was nothing if not enormously tenacious.

So she did the next thing that occurred to her. She pulled out our bikes.

It was late in the night, actually the wee hours of the morning. The roads were quiet with just a few passing cars.

Remember when you had your first bike with the tiny little wheels and the banana seat? Well, that was my ride in those days. It was purple with little flowery decorations and the streamers that flowed from the handlebars. That bike was built for leisurely riding to a friend's house a block or two away, not a twenty-three mile journey in the middle of the night.

I wasn't complaining much, but my six-year-old legs got pretty tired pretty quickly. I couldn't keep pace with my brothers' bigger bikes powered by their bigger, stronger legs and my mom on her 10-speed could cruise pretty easily. Mom realized I was struggling and had my brothers get on either side and tow me for stretches to give my legs a break. I thought that was kind of neat. It was a little scary, but also fun to be cruising along with my legs up on the cross bar, my hair blowing in the wind.

Then it started to rain. By now we were well into the trip and I was tired and now I was wet and cold. I had reached the end of my tolerance for this trip. I started to fuss and complain … then I started to cry. I wanted to be home or somewhere warm. I wanted to be horizontal. I could barely see, I was crying so hard. I was into full drama mode in just a few minutes time.

I will never forget my mom stopping us under an overpass where we would be out of the storm for a moment. She got off her bike and came over to me. I thought she was going to yell at me to stop the theatrics and keep going. Even at my young age, I knew she wasn't having the best night of her life either.

Instead of screaming at me, she held my face in her hands and wiped away my tears. Her words will stay with me forever … "Oh honey, this is not a crisis … it's an adventure!" and she smiled.

That was all it took for me to regroup and carry on.

I stopped crying and for the rest of the trip I was focused on the sound of my little tires sloshing through the water and the way the street lights reflected on the wet pavement. I was laughing at my brother's antics. I was still getting towed for stretches with a brother on each side of me and my feet propped up. Twenty-three miles wasn't so bad after all. I was in the moment and all signs of suffering subsided. It really did take on the feeling of a grand adventure!

That one incident really captures the beauty of my mother – and the incredible power of reframing a situation that doesn't meet your model. It's as simple as telling yourself a different story.

Was she right? Were we actually having a crisis or was it an adventure? It doesn't matter. The situation was what it was. She made choices that put us on the road on bikes in the middle of the night. That wasn't going to change. It was raining. That wasn't in our immediate control. My legs were short and my bike was smaller than theirs. Those are facts.

The only thing we had control over was our perception of what was happening. That was where the power in the situation lay. And that is where she focused her attention and mine. Viewing it as a crisis was certainly not helping make it any easier. Looking through the lens of adventure, however … well … that was powerful.

It isn't much different if you find yourself in a job that isn't your ideal. You know you would like to keep a roof over your head and gas in the car, but going to a factory every day watching fabric whiz by from one roll to another, looking for flaws, was never on your bucket list of things to do for fun. I actually had a job doing that when I was between business ventures. It paid the bills and allowed me to support my mom and my grandparents when they were unable to take care of themselves.

Was it fun to spend 72 hours a week in a building that smelled like fabric dye and engine oil? Uhh ... not really. Was I suffering through those days? No, I just made up different stories and games to amuse myself all day.

I wonder how straight I can get this roll of fabric to finish out? I wonder if I can beat my last speed record? I wonder if I can make it through this shift without a call to the maintenance department to adjust my machine? I wonder who I can talk to at breaks that I haven't had a chance to meet yet? Some of the workers had been in that factory for decades and seemed to hate every moment. I played with getting the grumpiest, most jaded ladies to smile at least once a day.

My internal stories and games allowed me to approach every day with a positive attitude. I didn't complain about my job. I didn't make excuses to slow down the work load. I was grateful to have it and doubly grateful for the overtime. Time and a half and double time are important when you are making about three dollars an hour and supporting four people with it.

In a nutshell, I showed up nice on a very regular basis. That is how reframing works. I just make up stories or games that work to keep me in a positive, nice frame of mind.

I was in that job for less than six months when I left to start my next adventure as a photographer at the resorts in the Pocono Mountains. When I left, the maintenance department made me a going-away gift of a dog made out of copper strapping. I still have it over thirty years later as a reminder of the friendships I made and fun I had in those walls.

Eckhart Tolle has a line in *The Power of Now* where he states "Everything is honored and nothing matters." This line had a profound influence on my world when I really took it in and incorporated it into my beingness.

What I take it to mean is that everything we do can be done from a place of being present and honoring the processes going on around us. And don't take anything ... and I mean anything ... too seriously. It's a way of tapping into the energy of the saying that we are spiritual beings having a human experience rather than the other way around. If you are honoring everything in your world ... would you say that you are in a state of constant gratitude? To honor is to appreciate ... yes? To honor may also strike you as being present in every moment of your day ... and maybe your night too. "Be here now" is something we can all do. Maintaining it 100 percent of the time is another story. We can strive for it. It is about progress, not about perfection. Would it also be possible to call it niceness? From my vantage point, yes! This is nice.

It also demonstrates how making up stories is a productive activity if it moves you forward. Honor everything that is going on around you and let go of the details that don't matter. The only thing that really makes a difference is answering the question of whether something is moving you forward. If the story you are telling yourself about a situation is holding you hostage, keeping you from taking a full breath or thinking clearly, it is your choice to change it to something that works for you.

That's nice.

Chapter 18

Screaming like a Banshee is Not Productive

Let's look at another scenario.

Let's say your spouse purchases a big-ticket item that you didn't agree on. He made this decision while you were at your mother's house a few hours away. In fact, by the time you got home, the 120" television was already installed! You had just agreed last week that you were going to make getting the credit cards paid off the very top priority until you were debt-free.

What do you do? Scream like a banshee on crack? Throw his favorite trophy through the screen? Call your mother and tell her what a no-good, slimy heel you married? Give him the silent treatment? Withhold affection? Buy something expensive yourself? "Great! I'll go buy that laptop I've been wanting!" Or do you just sit and cry?

Do any of these options pass the nice test?

If you choose one of those possibilities, would you feel better or worse? Closer to your husband or more removed? Does it enrich your relationship? Does it change what happened? Is your wish to build a close, loving and respectful relationship with your spouse? If your response doesn't move your relationship forward, than no, not nice.

What could nice have looked like? Well, you could have had a conversation prior to the situation erupting, but it's too late for that now. The money is gone. The purchase can't be easily liquidated. So now what?

Let's start with the premise that he knew you were gonna be less than thrilled with his purchase. Do you really think he was looking forward to the backlash? After all your years together, do you think he knew it was going to get a little ugly around your house for a while?

So what would make the choice worth it? Why would he go ahead and buy the TV if he knew he was gonna pay the price with you as well as strap you financially? What could possibly make it worth it in his world? You could certainly ask him, but there is a good chance that unless you change your mindset you are going to approach the conversation a little tweaked already and there is a strong likelihood that he is going to be feeling a bit defensive.

This is where we get to tap into our imaginations and start making stuff up. Yes, I said making stuff up! We're going to create a story to help center ourselves before we take on the elephant in the room or in this case the elephant-size television set dwarfed only by the gigantic cost of buying it.

Remember that our new story doesn't necessarily have to be true, all it needs to do is put us in a centered place to bring our best selves to the conversation we are about to have.

Let's look at a possible story in which he may be caught up. He bought the big-screen TV because the Super Bowl is approaching and he wanted to have a few friends over. Normally you go to a bar to watch the game, but this year he didn't want to do that. In fact, he remembers last year's game and he distinctly remembers that you looked so good he couldn't concentrate on the game because he was busy making sure no one hit on you when he was distracted.

Yeah ... that's a good story. Are you feeling better yet?

So he decided to invite a few people over to your house instead. He felt embarrassed about the size of the TV you already owned. (You do know that the size of a man's TV is tied directly to his sense of manhood ... right?) He figured he has been getting lots of overtime and deserved to treat himself. He figures he could pay this off in less than six months with nothing but his overtime pay. Not touching your budgeted money at all.

Now are you in a better place emotionally?

Maybe he was standing at the showroom just looking at the TVs when the salesman came up and immediately suggested that his buddies would be really impressed if he got that 120" Clear Motion Rate 240, UHD Upscaling and Dimming, Built-in Wi-Fi with Full Web Browser, Quad Core Processor in Precision Black and that's not all! It also has an immersive curved screen AND comes with a pair of 3D Glasses!

On top of all that coolness, this is the only one like it! The delivery truck was supposed to have twelve of these babies on it, but it was side-swiped by a herd of cows and all the other ones were damaged as the truck driver serpentined through the herd miraculously without hurting even one side of beef! Imagine that! Anyway ... the point is that THIS is the only one of these amazing, deliriously huge screens available within 250 miles!

What your man actually hears as he listened to the salesman was that he could finally get the better of Brock, the guy from high school that beat him at everything for four long years. Brock got the cheerleaders ... Brock was homecoming king and because he was so amazing they crowned him queen too! Other kids would fall over themselves to be in Brock's presence ... it was disgusting!

Your man felt completely annihilated by Brock in school and has been feeling less-than ever since. So here he is looking at this amazing television set and the idea the salesman planted takes root. This is it! Finally, something he can rub in Brock's face. There is no way Brock can beat him on this one! He's gonna be sure to invite Brock to the party. He cannot wait to see the look on his face when he sees this beauty in the living room. And the icing on the cake is that he will get to show you off, too. He can already picture you in that sweater that shows off your eyes and your other assets as well. Yeah, baby! It is gonna be sweet redemption for all those years of total torture!

How are you feeling now?

Can you see how your man may have gotten caught up in the moment and decided that you would probably be a little peeved, but you'd get over it when you actually saw this monument to his success? He may have actually decided in that moment that you would be proud of him for buying it.

He was so caught up in the moment it was as if he were under a spell. He became that 16-year-old all over again and all rational thought went straight out the window.

Don't we all have that happen sometimes? When we just revert into some earlier version of ourselves, but without the maturity earned along the way?

So … perhaps this has helped? Are you feeling a little empathy for this man-child you love? Can you remember a time when you made a totally irrational decision, consequences be damned! Maybe it was marrying him in the first place! Bwahahahaha! Just kidding …

Does any of this totally excuse the idea that he spent a ton of money on something without consulting you, knowing that you decided together that getting all your credit cards paid off was your new priority? No, it doesn't. Does the situation still call for a conversation? Absolutely!

If you were to go into that conversation with the idea that he did it just to tick you off, how will you approach the topic? My guess is you'd have your teeth clenched and your eyes shooting daggers.

Let's think about that for a moment … where do you figure that conversation will lead? My guess is that even in your wildest imagination, that conversation is rough water. I agree that it may feel good to get that off your chest … and I am not advocating that you don't … I am just saying there may be a way to get your point across without verbally annihilating the person in front of you.

What we tend to forget is that the person in front of us is a real human being doing his or her best – and the most heated and emotional situations are usually with people we care about.

So if you approach it with the idea that the boy just wanted to beat a bully at his own game and make you proud to be his girl at the same time, how would your energy shift?

This is all an exercise in getting yourself to a nice place before you talk. Why? Because it is much more likely to move you forward. That's all. It's not about ignoring the behavior or stuffing your feelings about it.

There are really tough conversations that happen from a place of nice. You can do anything sitting in that powerful place. You just get it done without the rancor and rot-gut that accompanies coming from a place of anger or disgust.

It moves you forward toward the important things in life. I don't know anyone who really wants to be in a relationship that is in constant turmoil and upset. (I do know some people that thrive on drama, but that is a different story.)

Remember, the story you tell yourself to move you into a place of love and acceptance doesn't have to be true! No … it really doesn't. The only requirement is that it shifts you to a place of centeredness. Seeing the other person's innocence as we proceed, helps keep us operating at our best, most loving and rational selves.

From this place, you can move forward and discuss the situation calmly. Recreate your agreement with new levels of commitment. Perhaps clarify the reason being debt-free is important to both of you. Look for the competing commitments before they rear up and sabotage either one of you. There are lots of chances to grow through this experience when we stay out of shame, blame and guilt mode.

We are all dealing with all kinds of programs and experiences that bleed from our past into our present and usually have a good chance of dictating our future as well. Some of those programs drive the bus without us being consciously aware of what's going on. It is said that we take our yucky past, throw it out in front of ourselves and live right into it … and then wonder what happened?

It's even possible that parts of our imagined story are true on some level. He may not be conscious of his competitive streak. Or that he is constantly seeking approval from others. He may be battling demons that say he is not good enough. Perhaps he is starving for validation and believes that if he has the right toys he will get it.

Remember that we are in the same humanity class with the rest of the people on this planet. We all came in with a divine and grand purpose and only two fears. (No … we were not born with a fear of public speaking. But good guess!) The two fears we are born with according to baby whisperers are a fear of falling and a fear of loud noises. Nowhere could they find a fear of looking bad in front of the cute girl or fear of solving math problems in front of the class. The fears we pick up along the way go a long way toward making choices that don't work to move us forward to the life we were meant to have.

Not nice!

Chapter 19

Imagination Nation

C omparison is a killer. It is through comparison that we annihilate our self-esteem. If we could only realize and appreciate our own gifts, there would be no need for comparison or self-flagellation.

Let's face it … that's why the question, "What would you do if you knew you couldn't fail?" is such an eye opener for most people. When you remove the possibility of failing, you remove the program that says "No! Don't try it! You'll fail and everyone will judge you!" If you knew there was no such thing as failure, what would you pursue? How much fun would it be? Learning to surf would be a lot more fun if you weren't focused on everything from how you look in that wetsuit to what if I wipe out and people laugh at me. Public speaking … just the thought of it moves some people into cold sweats and the shakes! Why? Mostly because we don't want to look bad. More than even looking bad, we don't want to appear anything less than perfect … ever.

If you are ready to play in a different arena, NLP is an amazing tool that addresses this exact issue on a deep, subconscious level and eradicates this and so many other fears within minutes.

Telling yourself a different story doesn't only work with those near and dear. It works with total strangers as well.

OK, so I'm driving along singing a song and someone cuts me off in traffic. I can make up a story that he is a selfish idiot who is determined to totally ruin my day or I can choose to tell myself that he's on his way to see his mom in the hospital because he is a very caring son and completely distracted with the news that his mother fell in the shower.

Poor guy! I really hope his mom is okay!

I can hear you now …. But that's crazy! He's a random guy driving like a jerk! You have every right to be aggravated. And furthermore, you know absolutely nothing about his life!

Here's the deal … if I do in fact get aggravated because I had to swerve to avoid hitting him because he was so close, who am I hurting? Does he feel my aggravation? How's my breathing? Did I get all shallow and rapid? How am I enjoying the great song on the radio now? How long do I carry that scowl and anger with me? I arrive at my destination and I am still ticked! Now I tell anyone who will listen what a jerk I ran into on the road! Yep … I'm gonna get me a posse of believers! I will tell the story with gusto and get people on my side! These are my people!

If I choose full-blown road rage and chase him down … well … hmmmm … what possible consequences have I opened myself up to? I'm sure you get the picture.

What if I see that he is still driving erratically? Now I'm thinking he may actually be drunk?

Same strategy. I just tell myself a different story … not for his benefit … it's for mine! Now I just add that some tragedy probably with his mother drove him to drink this morning … he doesn't know any other way because his dad is a raging alcoholic and it's all he knows.

Shouldn't you report him or something? Maybe he is drunk and going to hurt someone up the road. Yes … the incident should be reported. It actually is the nice thing to do. Of course the erratic driver may disagree with you … and that's okay.

You are in the nice zone because you are coming from a place of love … and concern for your fellow citizens and him, too. Who knows what is going on with him? And that is one approach you could use when calling highway patrol. "I have witnessed a driver behaving really erratically and dangerously … I'm not sure if he's been drinking or perhaps he is having a medical crisis of some kind. I don't want him to get hurt or hurt anyone else. Please hurry!" That's coming from nice.

You could also call the highway patrol and let loose on them. "There's a drunk out here on the highway that just cut me off and I had to swerve out of the way and I almost hit the car next to me! Then the jerk veered off onto the shoulder and back onto the road again. Where are the cops when I need one?! There he goes again! He's gonna kill someone if you don't catch him quick!"

Both conversations will get the highway patrol on its way.

So what difference does it make how you report him? Do you really even know which story is true? Could he in fact be on some medication that has him impaired? Have you ever seen a diabetic whose blood sugar is completely out of whack? Or perhaps he's having a stroke. Maybe my original story is the truest and he is really just in a huge hurry to get to the hospital.

How do you know how reporting it in the two different styles may affect how the police show up? What effect may that have on all their lives? As a general rule, aggressive behavior begets more aggressive behavior.

Again, it goes back to how you feel immediately afterward. Do you feel calm and caring or angry and ramped up?

If you feel calm and peaceful, chances are you stayed true to yourself and stayed in the nice zone.

Agitated and ready to chew nails? Not so much in the nice zone. Which state is more likely to support you in moving forward into your day with clarity?

The outcome is the same ... you have reported him and protected those you could.

Nice just lessens negative energy.

What it really boils down to is that it is always all about you.

Hmmm ... that doesn't sound very nice, does it? Sounds selfish, as a matter of fact ... probably because being nice is selfish. Selfish in that you are taking care of you. By taking care of yourself in this nice way, you are also sending out those good vibes to other people.

You are protecting your own energy and your own mood when you tell yourself stories that support your forward movement.

Here's a thought to ponder: if the Universe responds to your requests and places people and experiences in your path more rapidly and with more enthusiasm when you are open (staying in the nice zone) and that furthers you down the path toward what you were really here to do, wouldn't it make sense to foster that assistance from the Universe by staying nice?

Staying in the nice zone is a totally selfish act AND it also makes the planet a little more pleasant in which to live. So, why not?

Chapter 20

The Choice is Yours

W e make choices every minute of every day. This is a gift and it can be a curse. Things happen and we choose our reaction every time. So we are actually in total control. Some things that happen are less than magnificent. Although in reality they are all magnificent if you choose to look at it that way. Remember that everything is perfect. Perfect for your pleasure or perfect for your growth. And isn't perfect simply magnificent? Anyway … back to choices and gifts and curses.

We go through our daily lives and there are many moving parts all the time. From the time we open our eyes (or sometimes before) until the time we drift off to sleep, things are in a constant state of movement. Sometimes things meet our model or expectations exactly and we either acknowledge that with gratitude or we take them for granted. So the hot water shows up in the shower as expected and we continue with our morning routine … we may have actually had a moment of gratitude in that moment enjoying the feel of the perfect water temperature on our bodies ... OR ... the water doesn't ever get hot. R'uh roh!

Now is when we run full on into choice – choices about how we are going to react and what that is going to look like. It is the same no matter what the situation ... however big or small it seems to be. Are you going to stay conscious and stay in the nice zone or are you gonna flip and get nasty with yourself or those around you. Is taking a cold shower pleasant? Not necessarily. Is it the end of the world? No. The reality of life is that things are not always going to go as smoothly as you would prefer. You have the choice to either roll with the situation from a place of grace or feed the drama.

Which one is more likely to keep you on task to achieving your big dreams and goals? You already know the answer. Drama takes a lot of energy and doesn't help. You can still make up those funny stories for your friends later. You can dramatize the situation later for effect if you choose to get your friends rolling on the floor laughing. In the moment, it is usually more effective to stay in a place of calm. If you can quickly move to a place of gratitude ... well, that's even better. For example, the water is really cold, but at least I'm really awake now! Wow ... I'm really grateful now for all the times I stepped in here and the water was hot! Is this making sense?

So you move into problem solving ... but you do it with grace. No yelling or shame, blame or guilt. You simply choose how to solve the problem.

How much different is the conversation with your family when there is no blame going on? You just move right into options ... have the kids shower at the neighbor's house for school? Call a plumber immediately? Troubleshoot with tech support? Explore where you can find funds for the repair? Call and see if it's under warranty?

"But it is really messing up my morning! I have things to do, people to see, places to go! I can't be bothered with this!" I hear you and I understand ... these situations are not ideal ... it's just another growth opportunity staring you in the face.

Everything, everything, everything is either perfect for your pleasure or perfect for your growth. There are no exceptions! None! Water heaters that don't work or car accidents or marriage or divorces . . . the list is literally infinite! Perfect for your pleasure or perfect for your growth.

So ... is your broken water heater a growth opportunity or pleasure point? That may depend on how much you needed a cold shower.

Is it possible that it's both?

Perhaps the jolt of cold water did wake you up, fully allowing you to step into a place of gratitude for all the time the water was pleasantly warm, which gave you a new perspective on how many other things you take for granted in a normal day. What a great way to start the day.

Perhaps the water heater had been leaking for a long time, but it is tucked behind a ton of boxes in your storage room that hold your priceless baseball card collection. If it hadn't given up completely at that moment, you wouldn't have gone out to look at it in time to stop the water from ruining your collection.

Here is an old Taoist story that demonstrates the point.

"We'll see" is the story of an old farmer who had labored hard on his farm for many years, growing crops to feed himself and his family.

One day his horse ran away.

After hearing the news, his neighbors from the village came to visit.

"That's bad luck," they said in agreement.

"We'll see," said the farmer.

The next morning the horse returned, bringing with it three other wild horses.

"That's wonderful," said the neighbors.

"We'll see," said the farmer.

The next day, his son was thrown trying to ride one of the untamed horses and broke his leg.

"That's terrible." The neighbors agreed sympathetically.

"We'll see," said the farmer.

The next day the army came to the village to draft young men into the army. Seeing that the farmer's son had a broken leg they left him and took all of the other young men.

"That's good news," said the neighbors as they congratulated the farmer.

"We'll see" said the farmer.

"We'll see" is a story that means different things to different people. Some people say the story is about fate, or that everything happens for a reason, others say it is about experience and we should not jump to conclusions.

Perhaps the farmer sits on the fence with optimism on one side and pessimism on the other, and like him we all have the opportunity to see the good or the bad in just about any situation.

I see it as an opportunity to realize there is always more than meets the eye in any circumstance and we can choose to see every situation as perfect.

For example, many people have said that a diagnosis of cancer was the best thing that ever happened to them.

So many times our initial reaction to what we consider bad news is that we step into mucky drama-filled stories in our head.

A diagnosis of cancer is challenging to take with grace. And yet some people do just that. They accept what is, while moving forward with gusto. They accept what is and move into what now? What next?

A very dear friend of mine wrote a book about his experience with cancer treatment. It is hysterical to follow along as he has conversations with the radiation machine and lightens the day for the technicians and medical staff that deal with very sick people day in and day out. In a simple word, he was consistently nice.

Bill Raines has passed to the Great Beyond and is probably creating an atmosphere of humor there, too. Bill was a mentor, a friend, and a force for change in my world. He took living in the moment to a whole new level and his humor lives on. I have listed his book on my favorite list.

Chapter 21

Kids and Boundaries

What about kids?

Yep … nice matters. You want your kids to respect you? Be nice.

Again, do not be confused. Nice does not mean doormat. Nice when it comes to your kiddos does not mean giving them everything they want when they want it, if not sooner. You know what I mean … they're kids.

Nice when it comes to child-raising is not that much different from nice when it involves people in business or neighbors. It means going out of your way to stay level when things don't go as planned. It means not losing your temper when they do things that don't meet your model.

You know you asked them to (fill in the blank) and they didn't! How infuriating. Or not. Remember that kids are also humans who have much less experience than you. They are still doing the best they can while they juggle all the pieces of their lives. And that sliding scale is always in play. My son will do an amazing job of cleaning the kitchen one day … everything is put away and the counters are shining. The next he may totally forget pots on the stove and the counters still contain remnants of dinner. What happened? Shouldn't I expect consistent results? He knows how to clean the kitchen! Why can't he just get it done like I asked?

Well, there are many reasons why the results look different from day to day. Some of them very valid perhaps ... he only had a few minutes before he had to head to work, so he did what he could or his brother called and he went to go pick him up and totally forgot to finish when he got home, or his brain took a left turn when he started thinking about the cute girl he met yesterday.

Those would be reasonable. There are also other less acceptable ... he didn't feel like it and he figured you'd take care of it later. He told himself a story about how he didn't eat breakfast so he shouldn't have to do the dishes.

Either way ... the kitchen is not done as we agreed he would do. So now what? How do you come from a place of niceness while still holding boundaries?

Now that I think about it, why hold boundaries? Why not just be nice and clean it up yourself? (You know you were thinking that ... right? THAT would really be the nice thing to do!)

Because THAT's not nice! Let me repeat that ... because cleaning it yourself is not nice! That leads to all the things that doormats and their owners start feeling, resentment being right at the top of the list. Do you really want to run down that sad road with your children?

Ignoring the agreements you have in place is not nice. Children need boundaries to feel safe. A place with no rules or agreements is scary. Imagine driving down the road and there are no rules for driving. Can you imagine the fear every time you get in your car if you didn't know what was expected of you and you knew that everyone else driving was just going to do whatever they wanted? I know that seems like an extreme example, but I don't think I'm that far off as far as kids and boundaries are concerned.

So what do you do when the kitchen is not done the way you agreed to?

If you start yelling, what do you think the result would be? Would your son be happy to finish the chore? Yeah ... not likely ... at least not any child I know.

If you started to cry and talk to yourself about how nobody helps around the house and you are so tired ... would that get it done? Maybe ... depending on how soft-hearted your son is feeling. But will he be doing it from a clean place of love or through the eyes of guilt and shame? Doing it because you are crying may get the job done right now, but it may be setting him up for resentment for being manipulated. Guilt can certainly work, but it is a short-term solution.

What if you sat him down and had a conversation? What if you shared your humanness with your child and invited him to do the same with you? Is it possible that you may find some common ground and revise the agreement to make it more likely that you will both win? Would that be nice?

We want our kids to win!

And what is the definition of winning? Let's say it's to be in passionate pursuit of your purpose. Is that where we want our kids to be headed? Well, what does that have to do with boundaries and cleaning the kitchen? Wouldn't it make more sense to just let them do what they want?

They are passionate about other things … like video games and YouTube videos. They seem to think that's their purpose in life! Yes … yes they do … and those things alone will not move them forward into hot pursuit of their REAL purpose.

Here's where it could get interesting … who's to say that there won't be something in those videos that sparks an idea that leads to a passion? It can happen! My son happened to see a video about the treatment of animals raised for food and the conditions on which they live. Now he is vegan and seems to be super interested in health and lifestyle choices.

Anyway ... back on subject again ... why care about boundaries and chores when what you really want is for your children to find and develop their purpose? Because boundaries give your children the framework to fly and try new things. Chores – and more importantly honoring agreements – helps develop their character to live in this world as nice humans to be around. So in essence, chores and boundaries are nice!

Chapter 22

Kids and Agreements

Helping your children keep agreements is vital. Keeping agreements with other humans is nice and your children deserve the opportunity to practice. They will need your support and guidance. Even as adults we are often faced with choices we don't necessarily like after we agree to something.

Let's look at a kid scenario.

A child commits to going to a birthday party. At the last minute, another friend invites him to go see the Cardinals play. He really wants to go to the game! You can absolutely see his situation. The Cardinals' game seems like much more fun than a birthday party.

What do you do? You may be thinking … I could call the other parents and tell them my son can't make it because he's sick. After all, he really isn't feeling good thinking he's gonna miss out going with his best friend to see the Cardinals! So you're not really lying … right? (Has anyone else played those games in your head or is it just me?)

Is that really a nice thing to do? Your son in that instant would probably say YES! That would be nice ... he would get his way and not really hurt the other kids' feelings. What's wrong with that? No one would have to know. Well ... maybe/maybe not.

Even if they did not talk about it at school and it never got back to the birthday boy, there are at least two people who know ... you and your son. And what have you just taught him? You have established for him that agreements are open to be broken if it suits you AND that the truth can be manipulated to fit your own purposes in the moment AND that his feelings are more important than anyone else's AND that honoring agreements is just not that important.

Yikes! That's a lot of lessons in one swoop. Let's play those out when it involves you.

He makes an agreement with you that he will be home by 6 and he doesn't feel like leaving his friend's house at 5:45 to be home by 6 ... he may feel free to break it by texting you at 6:15 to say his friend needed him to stay because he was having trouble with his math homework and he felt he should be nice and help out his friend! His friend really was having trouble with his math homework ... the trouble was that he hadn't done it for the past week and instead of working on it he chose to play with your son.

So it wasn't really a lie … right? Wonder where he got the idea that manipulation of the facts is not lying?

So what do you do with your son and the birthday party situation? A conversation is required.

You could certainly just tell your kid he's going to the party and that's that. Done. This is probably the easiest option. "You're going to Timmy's party. Period! Why? Because I said so!"

I am not sure that will really teach him much other than that he has no power and no voice. That breeds victim-mode thinking and is not really conducive to passionate pursuit of his real purpose in life. Victims don't achieve big goals because they are powerless and they know it. Teaching your children to be powerless may not be your best strategy if you hope they will support you in a style to which you would like to become accustomed in your old age.

What would a conversation look like? Well … empathy would be broached. "How would you feel if a friend backed out of your party 'cause he got a better offer at the last minute?"

It could very well happen that after this part of the conversation, your son just makes the choice to go to the party and decides it will be fun.

You may also explore problem-solving opportunities, with honesty being paramount in the problem-solving equation. Is it possible that your son could call the other child and see if he could re-negotiate their agreement? SURE! You and you son could play with different scenarios for your son to come up with that may be acceptable. Maybe it looks like this … your son gets to go to the Cardinals and because he was missing the birthday boy's party, your son agrees to treat him to a movie with all the goodies next weekend. Or he agrees to deliver the boy's papers on his paper route for a week. Or he says he'll bake another birthday cake for him and have another mini-party next week after school with the other kids who have said they can't make his party. There are lots of options that may be totally acceptable to the other child. Your job is to help brainstorm those options with your son and come up with a couple that your child would be willing to offer if the other child is okay with him not going to his party. This teaches win-win … which is nice! It also teaches the value of negotiation.

The conversation also reinforces for him that you put a high value on agreements, a high value on honesty, and that you are on his side. It also creates an opportunity to spend time with your child discussing real-life stuff! That's really nice!

Chapter 23

The One You Feed

How does nice look when you are faced with aggression and anger …?

So we own a property outside of the developments that surround Phoenix. It sits on an acre and has all the things we were looking for in a home. The backyard is a dream and we love sitting outside watching the chickens scurry around the yard in a little pack … we love watching Cheyenne, the horse, grazing and being content in her heaven. The trees and the shade they throw are magnificent. I work in an office on the property so I am home most of the time or popping in and out. Everything was good in the hood for about the first year we lived there. Then, lo and behold, the property next door was rented to new tenants. Immediately, it became apparent that they had multiple large dogs that they chose to kennel right up against the wall that separate the properties. To say that these dogs are barkers is putting it really, really mildly. We thought at first they would probably settle down after a week or two. You know … new neighborhood, new noises, etc. No such luck.

They barked from what seemed morning to night, day in and day out. I'm pretty sure it wasn't as constant as I thought, but it was a lot! After about a month, Scott went to ask them to please be aware of the barking and either put them inside or put bark collars on them. He was met by the husband and the two of them got nowhere. There were a few ugly words exchanged, nothing terribly nasty, but absolutely no resolution.

After that encounter, the dogs were a little quieter, but ramped up again after a couple of weeks. Another neighbor called the property managers that handle the property and the dogs were settled down again for a while. Then they ramped up again! By now, winter in Phoenix was waning and the weather reached its pinnacle of perfection! Cool nights, warm days and lots of sunshine. Beautiful sit-outside weather. Great to read a book, have a chat with the kids . . . you get the picture. Only thing is …. yep … the dogs were on full bark mode every evening. Now what?

I hadn't yet met the neighbors. Quite honestly I was not excited to go over there. According to Scott, these were not nice people. I was afraid I would not get a good outcome and maybe make things worse. The stories I told myself were scary! They might reach over and poison the horse. They could have friends target our house for a burglary. They might start leaving the dogs out all night, too! I thought somehow they would make our lives completely miserable. Finally, after spending hours on a Saturday attempting to get the yard cleaned up for irrigation and listening to the dogs non-stop for literally five hours, I finally found my limit and headed on over. Scott offered to come with me as a buffer, but I declined. I wanted to have my own experience.

So I took a few deep breaths and absolutely decided that no matter what, I was going to stay calm and nice ... then I knocked on the door. An attractive, younger woman answered. I introduced myself and calmly explained that I had come over to have a conversation about the dogs and the barking.

Wow. I got a full tirade of defensiveness and aggression. I just listened. I tried to see her humanness and her innocence. I attempted to explain that I wasn't there to be nasty; I was just looking to find a solution so we could be good neighbors to each other. The response was no ... there is no solution because I am being unreasonable to think that I have any right to what her dogs do or do not do. Wow again.

I calmly said that I was not being aggressive; I just wanted some way to enjoy our property without having to hear her dogs' barking non-stop. No go again.

I asked if she had bark collars. She told me it was none of my business.

I asked if she could move them to the other side of her property where there aren't any neighbors on the fence line. No … the fences won't hold them and the owners won't let them put up new ones.

I asked if they could be put inside for part of the time. No – the house is too small to have four German Shepherds in the house all the time. It's okay for short blocks of time.

I asked where else they kept them when they weren't outside? In the garage – but it's too hot and the owners won't let them put air conditioning in there.

I was getting absolutely nowhere. I began to lose hope that I was going to be able to work something out.

I was told to leave multiple times. I stayed calm and restated that my only goal was to find a solution that we were both happy with. I just kept listening.

She mentioned that these were retired dogs. I started to get curious. What did that mean? Retired from what? So I asked. Well, as it turns out, she takes these dogs in that have been retired out of either the police service or the military and her job is to assist these animals in the re-entry process to civilian life. These are bomb sniffers and police dogs. Some of them have PTSD from their service. Others have never seen an environment where there is grass and cats and horses. Aha! Now I was getting to see the picture. It's no wonder they were barking constantly! And no wonder she was defensive. I was beginning to understand. What I still didn't have was a solution.

After spending some time talking about the dogs, I learned what the end game was for them after it was determined that they were rehabbed back into civilian life. (For those who are curious, they are re-trained as sugar-sniffers for diabetics, guide dogs for the blind, comfort dogs for those with PTSD and phobias, or just plain pets to be loved.)

I came upon the idea that if I only had some control of when the dogs barked I would be able to tolerate the barking much better. I asked if she was open to giving me her cell-phone number. The initial answer was no, because then I would just text her a million times a day. I assured her that I wouldn't, but if I did she could block my number. In the end, that was the solution we agreed to. I have her number, so that if there is a moment when I am at the end of my rope or if I just want to enjoy the back porch for an hour after dinner, I can text her and make my request. I also understand that there may be times she cannot accommodate me.

I was standing at her front door for well over an hour … always maintaining an attitude of cooperation and basic nice-ness while working to see her humanity and her innocence. I was determined to stay in my center and stay nice – no matter what she said or did. I will not pretend it was easy. When you realize that most people are doing the best they can with the tools and programs they have, it gets a little easier. In this case, she is doing something she has a true passion about and felt immediately defensive about it. These dogs do not deserve to be put down when they are retired after a year or two of service. I get it now. My tolerance is much better than it was and she seems to be much more cognizant of their barking. So far, I have not had to text her at all … other than to see if she could use some fresh eggs from our happy chickens.

As a follow up, we developed a good relationship. She would call if she saw something going on in our yard that seemed out of place and I ended up taking care of one of her dogs when they took a trip to deliver three others to their new homes. I never did have to use the power of the cell to have her quiet the dogs and I was actually disappointed when they moved out of state.

Speaking of dogs and battles …

A grandfather is talking with his grandson and he says there are two wolves inside of us which are always at war with each other.

One of them is a good wolf which represents things like kindness, bravery and love. The other is a bad wolf, which represents things like greed, hatred and fear.

The grandson stops and thinks about it for a second then he looks up and says, "Grandfather, which one wins?"

"The one you feed," the grandfather quietly replies.

Chapter 24

Competing Commitments are Not Nice

D id you ever set a goal and not achieve it? Even though you knew the steps and how much time you needed to get it done? You were serious about it. Dedicated and sure. And somehow it just didn't happen.

One possible reason is competing commitments. Very simply it means you are committed to more than one thing at a time. I can be committed to making more cold calls per day, but I am also committed to not appearing too pushy. I can be committed to a great relationship with my spouse, but I don't want to be vulnerable.

Competing commitments are the very things that keep us from achieving what it is we say we really want.

They are not nice. They stop our forward movement.

Here's an example of one that most everyone is familiar with, either for yourself or someone close to you. You want to lose weight. You really, really want to lose weight. You know that you will feel better and accomplish more in your day if you just took off thirty pounds. You would feel more energetic and happier being lighter. And your clothes would fit so much better! So great ... you decide you're gonna lose those pounds!

You do great for a few days. You're up early and exercising. Your diet is clean. No sugar or goop for you! You are gonna finally do this.

Then you go out to eat with a few friends ... you know you should order the salad with the dressing on the side and no bacon ... but then you see that the Chicken Alfredo is on special and it's your absolute favorite thing! You start the justification process. You know the stories you tell yourself. "I'll only eat half and save the rest for lunch tomorrow," "I've been so good all week, this won't hurt me," "I wouldn't want my body to go into starvation mode so this is actually good for me!" "I'll work out extra hard tomorrow morning," and the list goes on.

Then you realize that a glass of wine would be great with this Alfredo! And again the stories begin. Next thing you know it's two glasses of wine and an after-dinner liqueur ... now your resistance is in the tank and the cheesecake looks amazing!

So here you are the next morning feeling bloated and a little foggy. Your presentation is due this morning! Oh dear ... you were gonna certainly get to your workout after last night's eating debacle, but here we go again. You really should sleep that extra half an hour because, after all, work is important and you want to be clear-headed. Now you oversleep ... no time for those good nutritious breakfasts you've been eating. It's gonna have to be coffee on the fly. Starbucks is on the way to work anyway and they have a drive-through! Perfect! Now your stomach is growling. R'uh roh! Can't have that going on during your presentation to new clients! So you grab a muffin. You get the picture?

So here's the question ... did you really want to lose those 30 pounds? YES! Yes, you did and you probably still do! Do you know on a logical level that what happened starting with the Alfredo was probably not going to get it done? Yes ... you probably do. So what happened?

Your competing commitments totally took over the train and threw you off the rails. There are lots of competing commitments that may have played into the scenario.

I want to lose weight ....

BUT I really LOVE Alfredo!

BUT I also want to be social with my friends and wine helps take the edge off.

BUT I don't want to call attention to my "diet" by ordering "weird" with my friends.

BUT I don't want people to think I am a party-pooper by leaving the gathering early.

BUT if I lose weight I may have to buy new clothes and I can't really afford that.

BUT if I lose the weight my family will think that I think I'm better than they are.

SO if I lose the weight, my family won't love me anymore and my friends will abandon me, too.

Some of those may sound a little far-fetched ... but I can assure you they are not.

There are many examples of competing commitments getting in the way of what it is we say we want. Competing commitments can impact everything from your income to the quality of your relationships.

Many times just uncovering the irrational beliefs of your subconscious mind will launch you forward toward the result you are striving for.

If uncovering the competing commitment does not produce the result you are looking for ... then you get to do a little more playing with it.

You can replace it with beliefs that will move you forward. This is just another version of creating a new story that serves you.

Here are some examples to override the possible belief that "My family will ostracize me if I am thin and they are not."

~ I can extend my life and provide a great role model for my children when I get fit and healthy.

~ My family is just jealous temporarily and they will love me anyway when they see that I am the same person on the inside and perhaps my change will spark them into making healthier choices, too. My choices now may make an impact that will get me more years with my parents on the planet.

~ My family will be so happy that I will be able to climb through the access panel to finally get Mom's wedding album out of the attic!

You will absolutely find your own "reasons" and they will resonate with you on a very deep level. You will know when you found the one holding you back.

There can be more than one … you get to keep playing with them until you see the results! Then you will know you got this!

Competing commitments are just a form of bad story-telling that our brains use to keep us safe.

Not nice.

Chapter 25

Where Do They Come From?

Where do these limiting beliefs and competing commitments come from? The answer is anywhere and everywhere in your past and present. Some can even be passed down through generations.

Here is an example to demonstrate how and where some of these clogs can develop.

Let's pretend I have a burning desire to be an actress on stage. I know I can convey emotions and bring characters to life in front of an audience. I want to move people to feel alive and bring joy to the audience. I feel that live theatre is the thing that makes me feel most alive and I want to share that with my audience. People deserve to escape their day-to-day routine and I want to help them escape to a world of fantasy for a few hours at a time.

I really want this! But I am afraid to audition even though I know I am really good. I have studied hard under some incredible teachers and I do fine in front of the classes I'm in. I just can't make myself go to casting calls.

This is a competing commitment. I want to act AND I am not willing to audition.

Now let's take a look at where that competing commitment started. They are coming from a meaning we created along the way about ourselves.

This can be referred to as fact/meaning. Most of the meanings we created have their roots in our early childhood. We saw things and heard things and made up meanings as we went along. Everything we know and everything we identify are examples of meanings we created. It is as simple and basic as what we call the things around us. A chair does not know it's a chair and you would not call it a chair other than the fact that's what everyone calls that thing with four legs and a back that sits at the table that is only a table 'cause someone said so … you get the picture.

Well, there are other less obvious meanings we carry with us as well. Not all of these will be ones that move us forward toward our dreams. Those are the ones that can stop you in your path. Let's look at one that may be stopping our girl from casting calls.

Let's say that when she was five and in kindergarten, she was in the school play as a star in the sky looking at the garden growing. She practiced where she was going to enter the stage and how she was going to hold her arms to look like rays of light. She was excited! Deep in her soul, she has always had the desire to be on stage. This was

gonna be great! Every rehearsal was flawless. (Okay …
well as flawless as a kindergarten play can be. You've been
to these, right? Too fun and too cute!)

Anyway … the big day comes and she is ready to enter
the stage just like everyone rehearsed … except that the kid
playing the farmer didn't move back like he was supposed
to and his cardboard pitchfork grabbed the edge of her
costume and now she was all turned around. She couldn't
find the audience! So she started to cry, as any five-year old
might do under the circumstances, of course the audience is
watching all of this play out and is laughing because all the
children are so adorably confused and they love their little
munchkins in all their costumed glory.

She doesn't know this and she decides they were
laughing at her. She is devastated, runs offstage and sits in
the dark in the corner until they exit the stage. It's only a
minute or two, but to her it feels like an eternity. She hears
the applause and cries even harder. This was her big
moment under the lights and it's ruined!

The teacher finds her and soothes her down while
laughing just a little. Her kids were all so cute and all the
hard work paid off.

Her parents are sad to see she's been crying and do
everything to let her know it's okay. "Don't cry, Baby. You
were fabulous!"

So let's take a piece-by-piece look at what happened and what she may have made it mean. We already know that she is passionate about the stage and that rehearsals were fun. So let's go to the performance night.

There are facts and there are meanings she created to go with those facts …

Fact:

- She got caught on the pitchfork and got spun around.

Possible meaning created:

- It doesn't matter how planned it is … things go wrong.
- Other people are not reliable and I can get hurt.
- No one can be trusted.
- I can get lost on the stage in a nanosecond and I am not capable of finding my way back.

Fact:

- The audience laughed.

Meaning:

- I look stupid and everyone is laughing at me.
- My underwear must be showing!
- I ruined the whole play and it's all dumb now.
- I'm a failure.

Fact:

- She sat alone for a minute or two.

Meaning:

- I screwed up and now no one loves me enough to see if I'm okay.
- If I screw up, no one will love me and I will be alone.
- I am forgotten as soon as I am out of sight.
- I am not good enough.

Fact:

- the teacher was laughing when she found me.

Meaning:

- She knows I screwed up and thinks it's funny.
- She's happy I messed up 'cause she knows Suzy would have been a better star.

Fact:

- Parents said don't cry.

Meaning:

- My feelings aren't important.
- They must be embarrassed by me and my lousy performance.
- I am a failure.
- Emotions are to be kept inside.

I think that's probably enough for you to get the picture. There are infinite numbers of meanings we make up on a regular basis. Some of them move us forward … others hold us back.

So let's go back to our girl that wants to act on stage and can't bring herself to actually show up for audition opportunities. Can you see that if she never realized the meaning she created back when she was five that the emotion sitting beneath her desire to act may be what is stopping her from actually staying the course? Even though she has studied the craft and really wants to move forward?

She set up a belief system based on those meanings she created when she was five that is stopping her twenty years later. It is amazing what we will hang onto.

Of course, she doesn't know that's what's stopping her. She comes up with other things … she should lose five pounds first … a little more studying her monologue … her mother is in town, so it's not a good time … she couldn't get a cab … it was raining. These are all invented by her child-mind, her sub-conscious mind, to keep her safe. Because as we know … she has a belief that if she gets up on stage in front of a real audience she will fail, be unlovable and alone.

Let that settle in a moment … if she pursues her dream she will be alone.

Sad ... isn't it? No one was intentionally trying to squash her dream and yet the meanings she created from innocent behaviors around her at the age of five are paralyzing her from realizing her dream twenty years later.

So what can she do? How do you deal with old meanings that are creating competing commitments in your life and throwing you off the rails?

Well ... let's start with truth. Were the meanings she created true? Were they laughing at her? Possibly, but most likely they were enjoying the children performing in front of them.

There was certainly no malicious intent in any of the actions taken that day AND they are still stopping her.

Not nice.

To get back to the forward movement toward what it is she says she wants, she will somehow have to become aware that she is stopping herself. This means becoming very clear that she is the one responsible for the result she is creating. The result in this story is that she is not showing up for auditions or casting calls, which means she cannot get any roles in the theatre productions going on around her.

Once she establishes that ... she can begin to play with the idea of what is stopping her. There are probably infinite ways to excavate that information. One way is to do a gut check from a vision of herself where she wants to be.

So she would envision herself having secured a role in a production and picture opening night ... she is off stage and about to enter the drama on stage. It's her big entrance ... freeze frame. How does it feel? Does some of the anxiety pop up? Can she connect the dots from 20 years ago?

If she were to realize where the total trepidation started she could go back and create a different meaning around the facts from that day two decades ago.

Fact:

- The audience laughed.

New story:

- I am making them so happy they can't contain themselves! I am thoroughly engaging as an actress even when I mess up!

Fact:

- Mom said don't cry.

New story:

- Mom saw me even as a five-year-old as someone who was completely capable of managing my emotions. What she meant to say was there's no need to cry because we all love you, but if you want to you can ... she just didn't have all the words lined up because she was just so happy with seeing me on stage.

Quick quiz: Do the new stories you make up have to be true?

No! No more true than the stories you made up when the event happened. The only thing that matters is that it makes you feel lighter and more free. More liberated. Those are the feelings that will tell you that your new story will move you forward in your quest to live your passionate purpose.

That's being really nice to yourself and the world at large. You moving into your power and your purpose moves everyone forward!

Here's how you know it's time to start digging … you are not getting the results you say you want. That's all. That's it.

Feeling like money in the bank is a little low … where are your competing commitments? Limiting beliefs around money?

Is it possible that you believe that all people with money are selfish and greedy?

How about that money is the root of all evil?

You have heard that you can be rich or happy, not both?

So your goal is to increase your income by 50%, but you're not willing to make those follow-up calls because you think your prospects will think you are a nuisance. You're more committed to being seen as easy-going than to making more money.

Look for the limiting belief that gave you the idea that following up with people was annoying.

Perhaps you heard your mother complaining about a persistent sales person when you were little and from there you decided that you would never be like that!

Let's go back to "nice matters" for a moment ... one of the reasons to go back and find those things that are stopping your forward movement is because it is the nice thing to do for yourself and for everyone else too.

If that salesman were to discover that his mother's complaining tone was the root of beliefs stopping him from his goal, he could create a different story around that.

Getting the two sides of the competing commitment to agree is the very thing that leads to breakthrough and the ability to move into your pursuit of your passion with clarity and focus. That's nice!

Nice just gets you further faster than battling against the tide ...

Chapter 26

The Business of Nice

L et's talk about the business side of playing in the nice
zone. There is a perception that the nice zone may
play well in personal relationships, but business is another
story. My experience says differently. Actually, when you
think about it, what is business anyway? Isn't it just people
going about the business of life? So why would nice be any
different within the business world than in the personal
world? It's really the same.

Have you ever contacted a business and were dealt with
abruptly? Chances are it wasn't very pleasant. You may
have done business with them anyway, but it probably
won't bring up positive emotions next time you need them.
That is the difference that nice makes.

I think times are changing in business. Before the last
economic downturn (isn't that a nice way to describe the
CRASH?), money was flowing pretty freely. People were
taking second loans out on the huge asset they were living
in and everything was good. People were spending money
pretty freely. Business was booming. If someone happened
to call your company or step into your business place and

they were not happy with the greeting or the energy surrounding what you had to offer … well, to put it nicely …. you really didn't have to care. There was another customer right behind them.

Now things are a little different … people want more before they part with their money; more in the way of service and assurance that they are making a good choice. They know they have choices and they want to know their business is important to you.

I have a very simple rule I follow when I am spending money. I don't part with it unless the people I am dealing with are nice to me. If the company down the road is less expensive, but the company across town helps me feel they have my best interests at heart, I will go across town with my business.

That rule never fails me.

One more way to be nice in business is to share your less-than-ideal experience with the owners. Sometimes we choose to just move on to a competitor when things start to go south with a company. I propose that is not being nice. The owner is the one who takes the financial loss if his company is losing customers to the competition because of how an employee chooses to show up on the job. The owner deserves to know why.

Again, this can be approached nicely and without drama. It's information the owner needs, not a dramatic event. Telling the truth is nice.

What about your employees? Are they people, too? Well … the nice zone can serve you there, too. How much more likely are they to be in a good spot when dealing with your clients if they know you care about them as people and not just cogs in the wheel?

You say your employees don't really interact with customers? I believe they do … they do it through the products they are creating or the services they are providing for your clients. Just as important as those who are in front of the end user. They are the ones who will prevent those call-backs and returns.

Let's say you have an employee who is just not working out. You've noticed that he is lackadaisical in his work and is showing up late. He used to be enthusiastic and interested in growing with the company. Now it's as if he is just showing up to put in his time and grab that check. It's not meeting your needs at all. What do you do?

From nice ~ meaning you are in a good, centered space yourself, interested in moving yourself and your company forward AND assisting your employee in moving forward ~ you may choose to ask him honestly what has changed or what is going on that you need to know. Perhaps you find that he is having trouble at home and not getting enough rest. Or perhaps you hear that he is just bored with your business and actually the whole industry. What do you do?

In the case of him just being bored and unmotivated, there is the obvious choice of giving him the opportunity to find something that lights his fire elsewhere. In other words, you fire him. Let him go. Ask him to move on. On the surface, that may not feel very nice. And yet the reality is that as tough as it may be for him at first, you are probably doing him a favor. The greatest enemy of great … is good. Comfortable keeps us safe, but it also keeps us stuck! Allowing him to collect that check from you keeps him from going into hot pursuit of something that would really light up his world with excitement and passion.

Will he be happy to be fired? His first reaction is probably not going to look a lot like pure joy. Anger, frustration and perhaps sadness may come first. He may go into victim mode for a bit. You are likely to get the blame for blowing up his life. From that point, it is up to you how you react to the accusation and up to him how he moves on with his life.

So how is this nice? Nice is what moves us forward toward our dreams and our genuine purpose. Keeping him employed with you obviously was not moving him forward. You were actually complicit in keeping him stuck.

You were also in a place of building your own frustration which leads to resentment, which leads to anger and revenge.

You see that he is losing money for you and at some point you start to remove responsibilities from him and do things yourself. You need them done right! Your family depends on you to get your bills paid. Now you are doing some of his work, as well as yours. How does that feel? Good? Doubtful! Are you going to feel the same way about him as you did when you thought of him as an integral part of your business? Not likely! Are those hard feelings going to become obvious? Most likely. Depending on your personality, you may not make it obvious that you are angry, but there is no doubt that you are going to throw that energy toward him anyway.

Maybe you start doing things like not refilling the coffee pot when it's empty ... or closing your office door when you are on the phone. Or you start making sure that the only customers he deals with are those who are hard to handle. Perhaps you stop talking to him about anything other than work. All the personal stuff is off the table. Do you think he won't feel the energetic shifting of the environment? Of course he will. Again, he may not even be aware of what's happening on a conscious level. There is a whole world of energetic exchanges going on behind the scenes in our lives and they certainly do affect our situations. It's subtle.

That brings up the idea of what part of this scenario belongs to you. What part of it is a direct result of your own behavior and attitude? This is not a game of shame, blame or guilt. It's all about moving forward. What if you found that this type of thing keeps playing out? You hire someone who is completely excited to work with you. She shows up early every day with a smile on her face. She is looking for new ways to increase the profits and provides customer service like you've never seen before! Every phone call sounds like she is having the time of her life and the feedback is amazing. Customers love her! Then you start to realize that she is barely on time and drags herself to the coffee pot first before she will even speak to her co-workers. She starts slower and slower every day and you have stopped getting all the positive reviews about her performance. Soon she barely gets her required work done in a day. What happened and did you have anything to do with it?

Well if it happens more than a few times … uh … yes! It probably has something to do with you! It is probably worth spending some time looking at what you are doing or saying or implying that is causing your workers to slide down the motivation curve. And remember that how you do one thing is how you do everything. So if you are de-motivating your employees and co-workers, what might be happening with your children or your friends?

Nice moves everyone forward – always.

Chapter 27

New York State of Nice

S o what about native New Yorkers? As a whole, they have a reputation for being not nice. People from anywhere other than New York somehow have the impression that because their approach is a little different, they must not fit the mold of nice. I disagree. I believe New Yorkers are among the nicest people on the planet. You just have to know what they are saying beneath that accent.

I am a Long Island girl. It's where I spent the majority of my childhood. The accent and tone were all I knew. When I run into a New Yorker here in Arizona I feel like I am revisiting my childhood. I feel at home. I am also fairly certain that I am going to know exactly where I stand when I am with them. There is no pussy-footing around an issue. It's out there, on the table, ready to be addressed and put to bed. There is something refreshing to me about that way of being.

I realize that the tone of voice and choice of words can be intimidating to someone unfamiliar with the culture. So let me clarify by telling you a true story.

A neighbor of mine here in Arizona was planning a trip to New York City to tour a college with her daughter. As she was telling me the plan, of course I was excited for her. She was going to the Big Apple to explore. I assured her she was going to have a great time.

She didn't quite share my excitement and here's why. She was afraid of the "rude people" in New York City. I proceeded to explain that New Yorkers are the nicest people on the planet. You just have to know their language and verbal cues. I then gave her a possible scenario she may encounter.

"So Kathy, here's what's gonna happen. You're gonna be standing in front of your hotel trying to decide which way to walk to find the right subway to get where you want to go or the office where you're supposed to meet the counselor. You'll have a map in your hands and be looking up and down the street. A native is going to get close to you and with his very thick New York accent he's gonna say, probably loudly, "Hey Lady! You lost?! You're blockin' the sidewalk here! I got places to be!"

It's gonna sound like he's mad. He's probably not.

Before you can even answer he's probably gonna say something like, "Hey, you're not from around here, are ya? Where you trying to be?" This will probably be verbalized with great gusto and at eight decibels. You'll answer with what you're looking to find.

He will proceed to start giving you directions by pointing and gesturing and telling you all the landmarks to look for. "I don't have time for this. But, okay, so you're gonna go to the end of this block and go left. Walk up two blocks and there's a pizza place on the corner there. You'll know it's the right pizza place 'cause they advertise bagels, too. Who ever thought a pizza place would sell bagels? What's this place comin' to anyway? Their pizza is not bad, but what you really want is Joey's Pizza around the corner this way. My cousin Vinnie owns the place. I don't know why he called it Joey's, but he makes a really good pie. Anyway, when you see the stupid pizza place selling bagels, you're gonna go right. The place you want is half a block up on the left side."

You'll say thank you for his assistance of course, perhaps repeat the directions back so you're sure you know where you're going. You'll probably think he's done and start looking down the block in the direction he pointed. You may even start to walk. But the next thing you know he's talking again.

"Eh, you know what, I don't have time for this, but follow me and I'll show you where it is … come on."

Even that last offer may be said with a commanding voice and possibly sound like he's annoyed at the inconvenience. Rest assured, he's a native and if he didn't want to help you, he wouldn't. Plain and simple.

Then you'll be running to keep up with your new guardian angel that parts the sea of people for you and your daughter. While you're running behind him, he may continue his commentary on local sites you don't want to miss or the best place for coffee or share some insight about the school you're looking into.

So if you look at my definition of nice, this guy fits! He's helping you move forward to what you need in that moment. He may or may not be smiling, but he's helping you.

Kathy thought I was out of my mind. She and her daughter went on their adventure. When I saw her after their return, she just laughed. She explained that my scenario played out almost verbatim over and over again through the whole week.

New Yorkers are as nice as people anywhere else in the country; they just use different energy to convey it.

Chapter 28

Universal Law

Moving forward is not always easy. Staying in that nice pocket can certainly present its challenges and there are times when you may feel that things are just not working out like you'd prefer.

I thought if I could find a way to open myself up to the Universal power center, I would get much further than slugging through the mud on my own.

It's a lonely world when you feel alone and un-supported. I believe there is a power out there in the great beyond and the space between that is accessible to all of us. That power can help us move forward at incredible rates of speed. Did you ever hit one of those zones in your life where everything you touched turned to gold? You developed the Midas touch. Opportunities to dive into great projects fell at your feet? The perfect partners appeared out of thin air? You arrive at the store and there is rock-star parking waiting for you? The little things are lining up and the big pieces are just falling into place.

Author Napoleon Hill subscribes to the idea that there is a form of energy he refers to as "ether," which fills the space between all things. It exists in the vast space between planets where air doesn't exist. The ether conducts all vibrations from sound to thoughts. It also exists in the mind and the body.

How do you think perfect alignment happens when it happens? Do you believe those moments are purely coincidence? It just happens? I don't think so. I believe that the pathways between all of us are filled with this ether and your desires and needs are transmitted through it. The Universe is set up to serve you. And me. And everyone else on the planet. Maybe even to serve all the inhabitants of every planet in the entire Universe. That takes us on a whole different tangent, doesn't it?

Ether is like gravity. It's just there. It is in place and working all the time, like it or not. Gravity holds down that wine in the glass. It's hard to drink if it's floating around. Gravity also dumps that same wine onto your lap when you tip the glass over or miss your mouth if you happen to have had too much!

Ether works in the same way in that it is in place all the time. Ether is at work whether you like it or not. It connects all the energies out there and provides happy coincidence when things are in alignment; on the flipside when you're running late, you catch every red light on the way across town. This is an indicator that things are out of alignment.

The butterfly effect comes to mind. You've heard of this? The butterfly effect is the scientific theory that a single occurrence, no matter how small, can change the course of the world. A butterfly waving her wings in Japan can be the cause of a tsunami on the other side of the globe. This can happen because everything and everyone is connected.

This leads us to the law of attraction and the idea that we can attract situations and people into our lives that will propel us forward. There are lots of books on the subject and some movies, too. In a nutshell, the idea is that we each have the power to create our lives. The world we live in is absolutely a direct result of what you are attracting to yourself. The good, the bad and the ugly. The ether is the conduit that allows that flow to happen.

There is kind of an amazing mechanism to staying in constant forward motion … approach every single encounter, whether it be with a person or a situation or a class, with the idea that you are going to learn something amazing. That learning can be anything at all – a new way to bus tables to an awareness about yourself and your inner programs. It may be that you learn something about the world you didn't know prior to meeting and talking to that stranger from a different country. The point is that you stay open to the possibilities all around you. And one way of staying open is by …. yes ... there it is again … stay in a space of nice.

Do you know what the three most damaging words are when you are talking about growth and achieving those dreams? Here they are: I KNOW THAT. From there … it is an empty cavern of nothing new. No new learning; nothing can get in. So let me ask you something, if you knew everything there was to know about the path to achieving your dream life, wouldn't you be there by now? I have heard it explained this way. Have you ever read a book more than once? If you have, was it different the second time? Did you see things you didn't see the first time? Did the words on the pages change? Did the book elves come in and edit your copy of the book? Is it the Universe's way of messing with your head? I kind of doubt it. It certainly does illustrate that there is always more to learn and if you approach any situation or person with the idea that you already know what's coming … well … it is very, very unlikely that you will actually learn anything.

Have you seen the pie chart of what you know vs. what you don't know? If all the knowledge in the universe represented the entire circle, what you know would be a slice representing about 5% of the whole. These are things that you know that you know. You know how to tie your shoes. You know how to read. You know how to do advanced calculus. And the list goes on. Then there is a sliver of the pie of things you know that you don't know. You know something exists, but you don't know how to do it. Advanced calculus would fall in this category for me. Or perhaps piloting a sailboat. Speaking Chinese may be another. I know those things exist and have actually seen people do it, but I don't know how to accomplish it myself. I know that I don't know. This is about 10% of the pie. (Think about that for a moment. There are twice as many things you know you don't know than there are things you do know ... no wonder I feel inadequate so much of the time. I have so much to learn!)

The other 85% of the pie represents things we don't know we don't know. When you hear of something completely new it moves that thing into the "know-that-you-don't-know" category. If you learn the skill, then you move it into the "know-that-you-know" category.

For instance, in a business seminar I was exposed to Neuro Linguistic Programming (NLP). I was amazed! I wondered how it was I had never heard of it before. It is an amazing tool to actually reprogram your brain. It literally erases programs that are no longer working for you. So I now knew something I didn't know ... which moved that tiny piece that was in the 85% area into the 10% slice. I also knew that I wanted to know. So I pursued the path in front of me and started the certification training so that I could move that modality into the "know" category. Now I am a trained NLP practitioner and trainer. My clients get great results using it. That moves it into the 5% area. Got it?

This is one motivation for staying open to new ideas. New information is out there on topics and modalities you have no idea even exist. I am absolutely certain there are things that no human on the planet has moved to the "known" slice that are yet to be gifted to the planet. Who knew before Thomas Edison accomplished it that a flip of a switch would produce light?

Another reason to purposely stay open-minded is because it is nice. Can you picture being open and not-nice at the same time? How would that look? Most people are not exactly excited to share information to move you forward if you are being not-nice ... also could be called mean, nasty, sarcastic or argumentative. The names are many ... the feelings all come back to one – not nice.

Open minded is nice.

Chapter 29

Begin Again

Not nice repels.
Nice attracts.

It's really that simple. Basic niceness gets you more of what you want.

Nice speeds up the frequency around you and leaves you more open to receive what the Universe wants you to have. It wants you to have it? Yes, the Universe wants you to have whatever it is you want.

"When you want something, all the universe conspires in helping you to achieve it." - Paulo Coelho

Ralph Waldo Emerson said, "Once you make a decision, the universe conspires to make it happen."

I would add to those sentiments that being in the energy of niceness makes it easier for the Universe to show up for you.

It just makes sense. You will become aware of things that may have been in front of you for a long time and never noticed. Or you'll have a conversation with someone you have known for a while only to realize that they have the connections and the knowledge base you were looking for to help you get farther down your road toward greatness.

What you really want is bigger than the toys and the cash. It is your purpose and passion. Fortunately, pursuing your passion and purpose fully will lead you to creating the financial abundance to get the toys and the trips – and the shoes, too. With the abundance the Universe wants to dump into your life, you can also be part of solving big problems in the world.

You were sent here with a purpose and a passion that points to the very best and greatest good you can offer. You have the greatness within you … it is just a matter of letting it shine.

"Success is not the key to happiness. Happiness is the key to success." Albert Schweitzer

Let's take that another step. Happy people are nice people.

"Nice is the key to happiness; happiness is the key to success." Albert and Lauren

Chapter 31
Endings and Beginnings

Mom died in 1998 at the age of 61.

Her funeral procession seemed to be a mile long. That was pretty amazing considering she moved across the country from Pennsylvania to Colorado only a couple of years prior to her death and was already pretty much homebound the entire time due to her diagnosis. Where did all those people meet her? How did she gain that kind of fan base? She was a magnet of nice.

Mom was one of the nicest people you'd ever hope to meet. She had a smile ready every minute of the day. No matter what was going on around her or within her, she was present for you. When she was talking to you, you were the only one that existed. Her beautiful blue eyes didn't wander away.

She was never rude or curt to people in her world. She was pleasant at all times.

She rarely, if ever, had a mean word to say about anyone.

She loved her children with every fiber of her being and it showed.

She cared about other people and their journeys.

She was a wise woman.

Mom had more talent and heart than is even imaginable. I know I could be biased, but quite honestly I don't think so.

She was super intelligent and invited into Mensa. She was a brilliant musician and teacher who sang professionally while still in high school. She was voted Miss Congeniality in a huge graduating class. She taught piano and had two students she coached from beginner status to being accepted into Juilliard with their playing skills. She developed her own comic strip and was offered a position with King Features Syndicate to be a staff artist. Her cooking talents were tremendous. She was an exceptional speaker and comedienne. Bringing the house down with laughter was a specialty whether she was on a stage or in her kitchen. She was silly and she was fun. She was spiritual and valued her relationship with God.

Even in her final days, she would have people stopping in to see her from the crack of dawn until past sundown. Not to take care of her needs, those were more than adequately covered with home care and hospice help, but literally to sit at her feet and hear her stories and laugh with her. They would ask for guidance on the big decisions coming up in their lives and share their triumphs and excitement. The very young and the very old were engaged with her.

There was only one place where Mom missed the mark. She never mastered being nice to herself.

Nice to others is huge. Being nice to yourself is critical.

Mom was consumed with self-doubt and unworthiness. She was never willing to step into the greatness she possessed for fear of being judged. So many inner demons dragged her down and she never recovered.

I look at her life and see all of the places where she would have been headed to truly step into her purpose and her passion and she consistently chose the opposite.

Would discovering her passion have saved her from cancer? I don't know.

Is it possible that it would have changed some belief system and had her keep a healthier body overall? Perhaps with a little more health heading into the cancer treatments, her outcome would have looked different.

If she had become financially wealthy, would she have gotten an earlier diagnosis or higher-quality care?

Would her mental state of being have supported some of the alternative care she was pursuing?

Was there a treatment in Outer Mongolia based on the poop of a rare beetle that would have saved her life? I will never actually know.

Her death certificate says breast cancer. In my opinion, as much as it pains me to say it, I believe she killed herself. Through all the years of treatments of all kinds, I never really got that living was what she really wanted to do. I'm not sure that makes sense to anyone other than me.

Maybe her soul was ready to go long before her body was willing to give up? I just know that life was always a struggle for her and it felt like she was here on the planet under duress.

My belief is that the root cause was because she wasn't nice to herself. The inner voices of "not good enough" drowned out the voices of worthiness. Her self-doubt ate her passion and purpose. She didn't thrive or use her many gifts to their full potential.

She took it with her. That is a loss for many. I look at the lives she touched in the latter days of her life and can't help but wonder how many more she would have been able to move with her music and her art. Or she could have been a comedienne on a big stage using humor as a teaching tool, not a hammer. She could have been a speaker on faith and goodness and moved people to do great things for their fellow human beings. What books did she have buried inside that would have changed the course of some part of the population on Earth?

Of course, I don't really know what venue her passion would have taken her to explore ... but I know she's gone now. Her talent and passion and purpose are buried with her.

The last accidental lesson she taught me was that this life is certainly finite. This is not a dress rehearsal and there are no understudies to take your place if you drop out of the game.

It's now up to me to make sure that the lessons she taught me see the light of day.

It's in her honor and it is my privilege to pursue excellence and my passion each and every day. There will never be another me.

There will never be another you ... ever. Not with your thoughts, talents, gifts and passions puzzled together in exactly the same way. You're it! Make it rain!

Be your very best version of you!

And to yourself and others ... be nice.

Quick notes on how to use the power of nice to move forward ...

- **Start with yourself**

First and foremost, be nice to yourself. Stop the negative self-talk immediately. Take care of you. When you are feeling good about you, it is a lot easier to stop taking things personally and start moving into a place of acceptance with other people. You will not be as reactive. You will be able to see their innocence.

- **Tell yourself a different story**

We tell ourselves stories all the time. Most of them come from programming set in place long before we were conscious of it. Some of those stories drop us into resistance and suffering. Realize that you are in control now. Your new story doesn't have to be true. It just has to take the charge off the moment so that you can stay in a space of open possibility and stay nice.

- **Keep your agreements**

Keeping your agreements with yourself and with others keeps you in integrity. You can approach any situation clean and clear, knowing you have kept your part of the arrangement. When it is truly not possible, renegotiate as soon as that is apparent.

This also includes finishing what you start. That is where the satisfaction comes in. Doesn't it feel nice to finish the dishes? Or to turn in a project completed to the very best of your ability? Chaos and frustration are not nice (they do not move you forward) and that is what you have when you have a lot of dangling pieces, all left partially complete.

- **Hold yourself capable and accountable**

Believe in the power of you. You are not a victim. There is no power there! All power comes from the knowledge that we are where we are because of the choices WE made along the way. Call it being at cause or coming from a place of responsibility or any other set of words that resonate with you. The bottom line is that accepting responsibility is a great thing. It means you have the power to change, choose and move. Choose to move forward ~ always. There is a big world out there of things to explore and things to learn. Enjoy the ride.

You can have your excuses or you can have your results, you can't have both! There are all kinds of stories of people accomplishing incredible things. Homeless teenagers graduating as valedictorians. Dancers who are blind. Great inspirational speakers who have lived lives you wouldn't wish on your worst enemy. Stories of underdog teams that rose to great heights of success. Look up Nick Vujicic if you start to feel sorry about your lot in life. And the list goes on.

Hold others capable, too. It is not nice to buy into other people's drama or limiting beliefs! Hold the people you care about accountable. Remember nice is helping others move forward too.

- **Practice being in the now**

When you are fully present you will be able to truly connect with whatever is going on around you. As Dan Millman from *Way of the Peaceful Warrior* stated so beautifully, there is never nothing going on. Or Eckhart Tolle from "The Power of Now" – another amazing book. He states that from a place of presence "everything is honored but nothing matters." It's a beautiful way to live your life. Just that phrase alone, lived fully, will remove most of the drama that causes us to stop ourselves in our tracks.

It also leads to actually listening and focusing on the person you are with. There is real power in focusing on one thing at a time. And even more powerful is focusing on one person at a time. Don't you feel amazing when you are with someone who has all their attention focused on you! (Unless of course they have that kind of crazed stalker look … in which case, back away slooooowly). It takes practice. And it is nice! For you and the person you are focused on. You are much more apt to learn amazing things from this place.

- **Live life satisfied**

Gratitude goes a long, long way in the nice equation. You can be satisfied anywhere along the path of life. It doesn't mean that you are complacent. It means that you are grateful for where you are AND you are pursuing more/better/different. More money, better relationships, different business … always striving to improve and move forward. That's nice.

- **Smile!**

This is the most simple thing. Start practicing putting a smile on your face no matter where you are or what you are doing. It can be as simple as a slight turn of the lip or a full-out grin. Bring a look to your face that you are thinking something pleasant. That can be rainbows and butterflies or the way your child laughs when he sees a balloon. It is so simple. It truly changes the neurological set-up in your brain when you put a smile on that face. And you will be likely to get others sharing smiles with you. It's just good for everyone.

The Growth Company specializes in moving people forward. We work with individual clients creating lasting change from within. We also conduct workshops and trainings.

Lauren is also a keynote speaker when you are ready to move large and small groups forward.

Reach out today to discover what's possible.

www.TheGrowthCompany.net
lauren@thegrowthcompany.net

Resources:
Think and Grow Rich – Napoleon Hill
The Laws of Success – Napoleon Hill
If How To's Were Enough, We'd All Be Skinny, Rich and Happy – Brian Klemmer
The Power of Now - Eckhart Tolle
Postcards from Oncology – Bill Raines

Made in the USA
Columbia, SC
09 July 2018